DECLUTTER AND ORGANIZE YOUR HOME AND BUSINESS

how to buy, remodel and edit your space to profit and resell

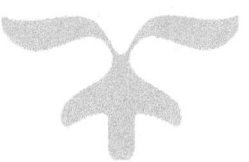

L. Keller

CONTENTS

BUYING FIRST & SECOND HOME

Chapter 1: Invest in Holidays homes 5
BUY TO RENT: HOLIDAYS HOMES 5
HOLIDAYS HOMES vs LONG TERM RENTAL HOUSES 14

Chapter 2: Total renovation of a VS home-staging property, with the ability to mask 23
DIFFERENCE BETWEEN RESTORATION AND "DISGUISE" 23
STEPS FOR AN INTEGRAL RESTRUCTURING 32
HOME-STAGING 41
SCALAR INVESTMENTS TO RENT 45

Chapter 3: Invest in 2020 after the Corona-virus 50
CORONA-VIRUS: COVID-19 AS A DISCRIMINATING FACTOR FOR THE ECONOMY 50
COVID-19 LETTER TO THE POSTERITY 54
HOW THE REAL ESTATE MARKET CHANGES FROM 2020 ONWARDS 57
SOCIAL AND ECONOMIC CHANGES 63
RESIDENTIAL MARKET: WHAT CHANGES 65
COMMERCIAL MARKET: WHAT CHANGES 72
AND IF TOMORROW THERE WAS A NEW "CROWN-VIRUS"? 75

Chapter 4: The ranking and identikit of the best forms of investment properties 84

CONCLUSIONS 114

STARTUP AND BUSINESS MANAGEMENT

Chapter 1: Business food & beverage and entertainment 120
WHAT IS A COMMERCIAL ACTIVITY 120
WHO IS THE SUBJECT THAT ASSEMBLES A COMMERCIAL ACTIVITY 121
WHAT COMES TO INSTALL A COMMERCIAL ACTIVITY 124
WHAT YOU NEED TO KNOW TO SET UP A BUSINESS 126
WHAT MAKES AN ACTIVITY WINNING 132
BUSINESS RISK 140
COSTS, REVENUES, EARNINGS 142

Chapter 2: Total renovation of a VS bar-staging property, with the ability to reprogram 146
DIFFERENCE BETWEEN RESTRUCTURING AND REMODELING 146
STEPS FOR AN INTEGRAL RESTRUCTURING 152
BAR-STAGING 164
SCALAR INVESTMENTS 173

Chapter 3: Marketing For Companies 180
DIFFERENCE BETWEEN MARKETING AND ADVERTISING 180
MARKETING POST COVID-19 183
CORONA VIRUS SEEN AS "GREAT MARKETING GENIUS" 199
MARKETING ACTIONS IN COMMERCIAL ACTIVITIES 201

THOSE WHO DO NOT NEED MARKETING.................... 210
MARKETING ACTIONS TO OPTIMIZE THE FOOD AND BEVERAGE SECTOR 214

Chapter 4: CONCLUSIONS................................. 258

BUYING FIRST & SECOND HOME

How to make short and long term investments, decorating your own house or organizing a rental property to profit passive income opportunities.

A guide to buy and resell

L. Keller

".think about your real estate business over 10 years"

CHAPTER 1: INVEST IN HOLIDAYS HOMES

BUY TO RENT: HOLIDAYS HOMES

In the previous years there has been a loud explosion of the concept of renting for tourism purpose, dictated by the news introduced by *Booking.com,* which was launched as website dedicated to exclusive for rooms to rent for hotels (so intended to professional organizations belonging to hospitality ground) then converted its offer expanding to private sector, with the availability of renting homes of owners and not specialists. With the arrival of Airbnb.com, the website keen to all types of private rents, from room to entire flat, from the boat to the camping tent, the concept has become decisively much more popular until coming up to be a proper and real trend and a real boom, so fast that not even legislative and tax regulations have kept up: initially there was not even an imposition of taxes well delineated by the rules that determine which subjects were deputies or not to practice this type of activity. Anyone found in the last three years had thrown into this type of business, buying houses, letting rooms or camper or any other thing, succeeded gathering savings that in some cases were real and proper "pocket moneys" end of month to cover the costs of bills, while in other cases it was converted into a second job or a semi-professional world where draw important gains.

But what happens when it swells a lot like a balloon and in a very fast way without being worried about how much is it blowing? It bursts.

For a couple of years, several municipalities, areas or regions, were struggling with the license war: as there was a regulatory hole or a novelty, they tried to repair by regulating the deputies of this activity, but making a huge mistake: they thought too big as utopia, without thinking about the reality in force. There had been bizarre legislations, architectonically unpractical and then the variations, between the licenses issued and those that should have been issued, with following legal trials: the result is the he result is that the profitability of holiday homes has collapsed even before they put a remedy on it, because the market runs faster than the bureaucracy, and those rules may be valid in a few years, if we are lucky enough to find ourselves in an another prosperous real estate economic cycle, but now is of very little use.

When I say that the system is collapsing I would imply that has happened what the analysts and we experts were bee observing: too many people who have secretly started to carry out the same activity together. Caution: am I saying that nobody makes more money with holiday homes? Absolutely not, on the contrary: there are people who earn will continue to earn because they bought using certain selection criteria that are always winning horses, and there are some organizations that will keep watching because they are well structured and they know how to present themselves, distinguish and evaluate their investment during good and bad times. But this book is addressed to small investors, or rather for beginners, so I have to worry about pointing out that, unlike in previous years, we will no longer be able to buy a random property, or the first one that seems to us to cost little, outside the area, without doing a prior study. That because, in a time frame of "fat cows" like before, with no rules, it was all worth; but changing the economic cycle, only the best and the most advantageous **quality / price for the customer** will advance and produce income, given that the demand will be significantly lower than in previous years. It is unquestionable, from interviews and videos that I had recorded in the last months of 2019 (even before the covid-19 emergency that hit the world and that will lead to important economic damages in all sectors and to decisive changes especially in the tourism sector) that I had however long seen advising my clients, owners and investors, that in 2020 the rules would change. As for the holiday homes, there were the signs and the first feedback from owners who began to sell their investment, in many cases only after two or three years from having assembled it. It was a suspicious attitude: why was a "so profitable" business with such an important outlay of liquids dismantled in such a short time? Has anyone ever believed the fairy tale that these people made too much money, but had they tired of this type of investment? All lies: when an investment really works there are **only two reasons** why an owner decides to sell: either he wants to maximize his profits, but then in monetary terms it is never a deal and you have to do your own thing well and predict whether in the in the long run there will be the possibility to amortize a possible purchase; or is lying and does not earn so much!

Bingo: here The reason.

The truth is that Holidays homes, in the long term, are a big deal for a big organization or, in the contrary, it is a great deal for "the madam Maria" who in her free time leases a room in a basement in time to pay for the light, but they never have been and will never be for a common investor. Given that all still are living over the moon and still thinking of buying a house with the famous "100.000 euro of the grandpa" (amount often out of market that represents sometimes just four auto places or a mini flat in a big city; in outskirts it is allowed the purchasing a full modest house), you must absolutely study and perceive that there are some fixed prices not indifferent when it about buying and reselling real estate properties and above all there is a dispute on the on the repayment of the cost that surely requires you to think about **your business over a period of at least 10 years.**

Ten years? But if the boom of the Holidays homes blew up and it is deflating in less than 5...

Of course, in fact except the two cases mentioned above, for all the rest it is been just a trend or a soap bubble, because who does not have a clue to see in the right time when there were deflated pieces or who was thinking of making out of it a lasting life is getting prepared to survive during harsh times. It must be said that who bought in relevant or main positions, I mean sea view, forefront of walk or close to symbolic areas, in centre or any level of property and special features (attics and city houses, very rare commodity), will never lose anything of its equity! But instead who invested in unidentified places, guided by the only one discriminating to buy at a low cost, if he has lost *the train of favourable economic cycle,* he will encounter many problems in the new year both in selling, and continuing with this type of rent. Remember always that, in our analysis we always take into account subjects that undertake an activity with all the permissions and the respect of rules, therein including tax and contractual ones. In statistics are not included those that operate from the borders allowed by the law or with non-legal devices, aimed to stay afloat and so they are unauthorized or illegal to work.

Common holiday homes or low quality so therefore a drop in productivity due to the decrease in the market in general, but also to the strong recovery of the Middle East, which at the moment seems to have smoothed out the conflicts of the past years and which has always an attractive appeal. A careful observer saw the signs of a radical change in investments for various reasons regardless of the events on the holiday home, just looking at the general context: we remember the crisis of tour operators who in 2019 lost two giants that moved millions of people worldwide: this has had a direct impact on the prices of airline tickets, which have increased for certain destinations until reaching inaccessible figures for certain periods; closure of air bases and change of policy of the main airlines. As if the reasons already described were not enough, we can also mention the consequences of *Brexit* which in the coming months or next year will lead the British to analyze the opportunity to have a second home and a lot of taxes to pay, or sell, and then enter new properties on the market (which will add to those already physiologically present for family reasons, to abandoned holiday homes and to all those that will be sold for various reasons and logics related to the market). We always keep in consideration the new constructions, many of them, because we will quickly pass from a production cycle to a recession, even more drastically after the advent of the *covid-19*, something of which nobody in the world had had any warning.

The result: a lot of competition which will lead in a reasonable time to a **significant drop in the value of a property** and therefore in the sale price.

But let's go back to our little investor. The advice is obviously not to invest in holiday homes in these conditions, but the input is instead to "be ready to invest". The *rationale* is that you don't necessarily have to do the same thing: the holiday home system has been completely saturated in a few years due to the disproportionate increase in supply and demand that has become increasingly demanding, impressive, for those who wanted to fill the dates, to be more and more competitive, to lower prices and therefore to obtain less earnings. In fact, those who survive this system now in recession will be the organizations that have been able to vary and work in scalar form on different areas and types, the private individual who has purchased a truly unique property or precisely "Madam Maria" who will be happy to pay some small shopping. All the others, who did well on the distance, between the time they spent in managing the guests, and in the type of life they used to endure, to derive what in the end is "a misery", removed expenses such as portal fees and commissions, and management fees such as purchases, reforms, cleaning and maintenance. Anyone who ventured into a detailed calculation of his investment, remember that, net of this, it must always be taken into account that during the purchase phase expenses were paid such as taxes on the purchase of real estate and notary registration that are not indifferent. During the sale stage, the agency's cost could be incurred (which, however, when it is good, can offer a competitive service, which as we will see later, saves real money; moreover, whose invoice for the performance is **fiscally deductible**), and a series of costs that everyone underestimates also because most of them are subsequent to the sale and arrive, as a surprise even up to a year later: these are the fearsome *sales taxes*, which range from the closest territorial tax of the municipality to which the properties, up to the incidence in the tax return, where there will obviously be to declare *income for the sale of the house* with absolutely important percentages, based on the calculation of the much desired income (which is why it is often useless to try to inflate the prices as much in the resale phase, to then have unlikely gains, on which taxes must be paid later). If there is a capital increase, due to this type of revenue, there will be taxes to pay: clearly for a seller it will not be good news, also because most of them do not take it into account, insisting on slowing down the sale of their motionless, looking for an ideal profit, which will not be such in reality. In summary: "why, apart from in rare cases, is the holiday home not a huge investment? (unless done in a professional and scalar or peculiar way)". Because on the basis of long-term depreciation, *remove the expenses before, remove the expenses during, and remove the expenses later,* when you pull the line, if you went even or "brought the loaf home", there is to be very satisfied (not forgetting also the "lost" **time and resources** that could be dedicated and invested in other perhaps more productive activities).

HOLIDAYS HOMES vs LONG TERM RENTAL HOUSES

So what are you advised to buy if this model is not profitable in the long run? The answer is simple. As there are *trendy* goods, as is the case with safe assets as it happens with the Stock's shares: the holidays are a *trendy* good that allows to use the rents of high yield, but they are an operation of high risk, if is analysed the whole investment. Actually you have to offer a high standard, win the ruthless competition and make a speculative planning very targeted scale to differentiate the investment. The safe asset, that is which is advised to invest in without making any mistake ever, is the house to rent in the **residential area**: that is not uncommon that people buy or rent a house to *live in*. it is not a novelty, it is not *trendy*, but first of all it is safe. In second place, it is climbable. Then if you want another series of reasons to know the profitability of renting for a long period, we can mention that is an investment with liabilities entries, which means once well chosen (and not wrong!) the profile of the room tenant, and established the contractual system, no longer requires any type of day-to-day management. Then if you want to stay more safe, you can organize yourselves with some insurances on the property or even on non-payment of the rent. With these cautions you will have a solid business, in full operation, recognized by the bank in terms of revenue, at the time of requesting a mortgage for an another investment and absolutely encouraged by any state law, which proposes a much more favorable taxation with respect to the activity of holiday homes. In certain geographical areas, then, the demand for long-term rents is so high, that there is not even much competition, and therefore good returns can be obtained in absolutely favorable market conditions.

You will avoid in this way to have a staff or to intervene to check in and check out at any hour of the day and night, with frequent delays and misunderstandings. You will avoid housekeeping and the need of always being competitive every week, and you will be able to dedicate yourself another job or plan another investment so this can walk up itself. Does it make less? Yes, but this model of business applicable and prosperous *from the dawn of time:* indeed many will object that last years the revenue of holidays cottage was definitely superior: except that it is questionable, since residential rents had also grown to hyperbolic numbers, and apart from that we have already argued that the calculations are not made only on inputs and on the short term, but on **costs-revenues and long term**; in any case I can argue very strongly that something that has existed for years and years cannot be compared with something that has worked for a few years and of which we already see obvious limits. If, however, there is someone who is not of the same idea, given all these clear arguments, he can safely continue on the trendy line, knowing that however it is called "risk" and as for definition, it does not exclude the possibility of significant losses of capital and time, unless you have the strength to do it in a structured and scaled way.

Finally, I propose a truly innovative, but less risky, idea. This is my personal *rental income* model which is not absolutely connected to holiday homes, but neither is it a traditional rental model. I'm talking about using a regulatory hole and working in legality, aware that it is *border-line* but at the moment always on the correct side. I'm talking about a model without competition with easy management and sustainable costs, and perhaps even with better prices than traditional rental (even if not comparable to the gross income of holiday homes). I am talking about medium term rent or **seasonal rent**. I propose this model as an investment of the future, suitable only in certain areas, because it combines, in my opinion, all the advantages of long-term rental and many advantages of the model of holiday homes, without however having the same burdens and defects.

In fact the seasonal rent, which by definition could be for example for 4 or 6 months, according to the general norms of the operating area, it does not include any competition game: let's think about for example hotels that do not have any intention to compete with this type of customers because they do another type of profession. If for example you try to ask a hotel to rent a room for six months at a preferential rate, many will tell you that is anti-economic and it does not fit the hotel's policy. In case of holidays homes, instead the hotels have something to say and object: those are doing the exact job of a hotel and by definition there always will be competition ad war in place between two realities. instead, we plan now to work only 3 or 4 customers a year to rent our property: they will have a contract of several months and if they want to stay longer, for their needs, most welcome. With due attention and changes, the current legislation will be adopted in the long run in the absence of specific legislation, with relative taxation, and there will be no need to depend on a portal (*Airbnb and Booking* have important service fees) to find the customers. Let's think to all tourists of a sea zone, for physical or relax reasons they decide to spend an extended stay. Think about the case of some countries where who can afford for work reasons, find more beneficial to move for six months in an area with a very mild climate instead of switching on the heating during the long Scandinavian winter or the British one for instance. But then we may think about who migrate from the original country looking forward an occupation, that perhaps does not still have the documentation or job requirements to guarantee a long term rent, but he got some savings that guarantee or cover few initial rental months. Think of who is building a house or who "sells to buy another house" and who would gladly rent something in the medium term, and dozens of other cases. **There is a whole market and there is no competition.** As in all investments, however, the right move must be made at the right time and the location and type of property must not be wrong. Enough with the hunt for the most bizarre purchase just because it had a low cost: that was the mantra of the holiday home, in the boom period; an investment of fashion, unstable and therefore speculative. We must therefore differentiate and understand which is the good property and which is the least good property. If you do not have knowledge of the area, the most advisable thing is to rely on the best professional on the square, who is not the one who necessarily wants to sell us something, but is the one who understands the needs of an investor buyer according to the plan managerial that he has drawn up and communicates to him. Once the property has been identified, negotiated and purchased, it must then be put in a position to produce revenue, i.e. prepare it, so that it can be rented in the medium or long term, respecting certain medium-high quality fees which are essential to be competitive in 2020.

For this reason we will see how to completely renovate or arrange the house we have just bought "in good condition", only in certain cases, to make it a productive investment.

"Either the renovation and the *home-staging* have some well-defined rules and equilibriums"

CHAPTER 2: TOTAL RENOVATION OF A VS HOME-STAGING PROPERTY, WITH THE ABILITY TO MASK

DIFFERENCE BETWEEN RESTORATION AND "DISGUISE"

Turning to our first-time investor, I cannot fail to explain to him exhaustively the difference between carrying out a total renovation of a property, or giving him only the classic "touch-up". Obviously everything depends on the actual initial condition in which the property is located, on the regulations in force and on the project that he thought of in the long term. It is clear that, to acquire a holiday home license, there are stakes and parameters and certain standards to follow, while in long-term rent we say that these are comparable to the appropriate and current rules of any residential home. But when in any case we decide to intervene, we will have to plan a further investment to put the property in ideal conditions: it is good to understand when it is convenient to renovate everything (and when not), depending on the case, from an aesthetic and use, but above all from a financial point of view.

Let's start with the reflection that a long-term investment always deserves an important and massive investment, as opposed to a speculative investment, whose profit is high only if the costs are contained (another reason why you don't see the meaning of many operations with unlikely and unlikely holiday homes, with renovations that will never be amortized). An investment that lasts over time always deserves a suitable adjustment, therefore, if it were a customer who has bought an inactive house for some years, with my eyes closed I would recommend a total renovation, while to the customer who wants to speculate I would absolutely say to rely on the best professional of home-staging of the area and trying to do everything with the strongest imagination and taste, but with the least possible outlay.

What is a home-staging professional? I could simply compare it to the makeup artist of a famous artist: he must work with what is there, preserving the soul of the subject, saving the substantial and characteristic features because he cannot afford to change deeply; however, he must give significant strokes that, while maintaining the same substance, hide the defects and enhance the qualities, adding secondary elements and accessories that enhance the characteristics and the new personality that you want to attribute to the subject itself. It is practically the art of using what is there and a few other new resources, reorganizing them, combining them and obtaining a new, dynamic and original mix. Clearly it has different costs compared to a total restructuring and it absolutely does not solve the problems that a more massive investment can solve. However, it helps to improve the perception of an environment, to make it more pleasant and updated and to give a change of atmosphere; if well studied it can be equally radical. The two techniques (renovation and home-staging) can also be partially combined, and this is what we normally try to do in properties that have a good base and that need only be updated to the 21st century; the typical example is that of a house that is good for floor installations and distribution, but has no consistency in the placement of furniture, colors, and perhaps some separators. Normally we intervene to renovate the kitchen and bathroom area and to proceed with a home-staging for the other areas, to recover and save the salvable and then give a coherent and dynamic final touch to the whole house. The problem is that almost all vendors are convinced they have a coherent and organized home, when in reality it is almost never like that. Most of the time, in fact, the house is organized but exclusively according to a completely personal taste and logic, which however do not match the needs of the majority of common sense people; therefore, even if in that house the seller is convinced that he is comfortable, depending on the circumstances, it may even become bizarre or useless for the users of the buyers' market. So, the first thing to do is to realize, when buying, if a house needs to be renovated and to what extent, so as not to find yourself with some nasty surprises at a later stage. Often who sells a house, whether private or agent, is not an expert in renovations, and this can be a problem because when the buyer is not as well, expectations are created very easily which are then not met; the consequence is to find oneself with important cost increases for the buyer who, in order to have a truly functional property, is forced to resort to important extra budgets. Another problem is that in today's time, anyone, inflated by the big bubble of holiday homes, is convinced that he is the greatest expert on renovations ever, when instead often he does not know the legislation, he has no foundation of architecture or he does not collaborate with expert people and thinks that buying some weird furniture at the supermarket is knowing how to furnish a house. Both the renovation and the home-staging have well-defined rules and balances and those who do not respect them often find themselves with a poor quality end product and therefore poor durability, or worse with problems or with a final product rather botched and inconsistent. So to speak, he finds himself with crap made by an amateur, without soul or balance.

One thing not to be underestimated are the implants, before deciding what type of intervention to apply. We must always remember that for the "new" regulations (which are no longer new because they have been in force for years), the electrical system must comply with the regional parameters of the supply companies and is subject to the design and signature of a specialized technician: this means that there is no do-it-yourself. Of course, if a system needs to change a couple of sockets, nothing happens, but in the event that an increase in power, a change of contract or some substantial variation is requested then the administration company could be denied, demanding a complete reform of the system same: big problem if it had not been evaluated and detected during the purchase because what seemed like a detail means, translated in a nutshell, that a lot of things must be changed and restored:

- break the floor for the whole house, to trace the new light points and switches

- pass the electric cables and close the floor

- cover the floor with a new surface because the material will not be the same as the front one

- change the electrical panel

- request compliance from the specialized technician and therefore increase the power

A nice grain for those who thought they had bought an apartment that had a beautiful floor and there seemed to be little to do. Translated into figures, we are talking about thousands of euros and the different time needed. So for consequent reasoning, the high price of that house, motivated by that beautiful floor, which seemed everything in order, is actually a surcharge, because it will have to be changed a lot to make it functional. In fact, compliance must be signed and guaranteed and could be subject to control; so either everything changes or nothing changes and these are economic evaluations that must be made before a purchase, because otherwise the solution of many is do-it-yourself (perhaps changing only a part and looking for gimmicks for compliance), or resign yourself and get annoyed every time the power goes out, because we have attached a lot more equipment to it than what the system was designed for. Not to mention the costs of the administration when you go beyond the parameters. Many even in a nice apartment decide to opt for the division of two rooms and prepare double kitchen, double lights, double everything: pay attention to what you pay for this type of house, because in this case, if there is to enhance the electrical system, that the property is more or less in good condition rather than completely to renovate, it changes very little, because you will have to touch almost all of it; so it is almost not worth buying something "almost ready" and paying it for an evidently high price, if you then have to intervene to redo almost everything.

With the water system you can get cheaper, even if the same principles still apply. The pipes must be passed according to the standard for the ceiling and must be in PVC (the typical green ones that have replaced the typical ones of an antique copper color), which are now non-compliant, because they are subject to easy oxidation. "We can get away cheaply" if they have become very beautiful, so where there was already a false ceiling and then you can cut that and run the pipes in there: it has important labor costs, but at least not excessive for the small material. Or it is quite reasonable, in case the problem was solved by covering the pipes with frames or channels. Clearly it is absolutely inexpensive for those who leave the pipes in view, but aesthetically it is not a solution that can contemplate, unless it is perhaps a commercial space, where you can play with the commercial style or a residential style house urban.

As for the TV and internet and telephone installations, it should be noted that they are the things that most worry users, while in reality they are the simplest, least expensive and fastest to install, according to the company chosen and with their own assistance, and honestly there is something else to worry about as investors struggling with a restructuring; in fact, once verified that in the area or in the building there is the desired telephone / internet signal and the parabola or antenna with the desired digital or analogue reception, with a phone call to the service administration company everything is resolved.

So when you are aware of the real state of these technical parts and any problems or options in the change of distribution of the internal divisions of the various rooms of the house (it is not secondary to know which walls are the main and cannot be touched and which instead they can be "moved": this operation must be planned and carried out by a sector professional according to a new design, respecting current laws and building rules), then we can finally decide whether to intervene with an integral reform or with a touch-up. Otherwise many times the saying applies: "it is not always beautiful what looks beautiful", because it could be everything to throw away. There is an unwritten rule in this sector and it says "be careful before buying what you need to restructure and what you can really save", because when you start applying changes, and they start to be different, you end up restructuring everything anyway, even if it wasn't expected; partly because of the desire to have something well done, partly because when a person "makes 90", instinctively they are led to make "100 round digits". In the end, if you have not made a good plan, and a correct assessment of systems and costs, you always end up systematically doubling your expenses.

This is why there are professionals and **professionals in the real estate sector**: when working with a good collaborator, they will be able to foresee and intuit these situations; on the contrary, those who do not have this type of training attached, are simply a normal mediator.

STEPS FOR AN INTEGRAL RESTRUCTURING

We have already seen how the first step is absolutely an analysis of the state of the property, not according to aesthetic criteria, but according to the expected updates necessary in a long period for the installations.

Below are the most significant steps of an integral restructuring, the order of which is by no means secondary, because many times, who is not an expert in this sector, starts for half or for the end and then must go back to correct or redo what had to be done in another way; needless to say, in doing so there is a huge increase in time and costs and often jeopardizing the previous work or the final result.

- **Check the current regulations:** with the help of a professional, contact the municipality of residence to request the necessary permits for the intervention. Through technical advice, define criteria and rules and what can be done (and what can't), at the structural and plant engineering level. It is absolutely essential, in order not to risk making irreparable mistakes, to work authorized and in peace and to have clear ideas also in terms of costs and project. Recommended inspection for all technicians who will have to work: architect, master worker, electrician and plumber.
- **Study the new distribution of the rooms:** compatibly with the project, first of all define where the technical spaces of the bathroom and kitchen are located, and then concentrate on the main rooms such as lounge or terraces or leisure space. Lastly, carefully check the location and size of the bedrooms, then going over everything from the beginning and checking that there is consistency and the right compromise between aesthetic beauty and practicality. It is necessary to be very clear where to locate sensitive spaces before starting work, because

all installations depend on it and, cascading, realizing a mistake late can be impossible to solve or very expensive.

- **Demolition:** it is the first active phase of the work. We will have already studied whether there are old walls to be demolished or old installations to be abandoned. At this stage it is appropriate to protect or remove the furniture and parts that you intend to save, so as not to damage them because it normally produces really annoying dusts at the time of cleaning and inconveniences due to the work of several people in the same environment. It is appropriate to clear the area as much as possible to facilitate the work and then be able to easily intervene in the removal of doors and fixtures or demolition of walls, decommissioning of furniture that does not interest and anything else. If the wooden floor, for example, is one of the things that can be saved, protect it to avoid direct scarring for moving furniture or even unwanted, for the simple passage with the possibility of small debris under the shoes. • Construction of new walls: if provided, there will be the redistribution of the surface with new walls that will delimit the new size of the rooms. According to the uses, they can be made with blocks, with wood or with the most economic and widespread solution and with the best aesthetic result: the plasterboard, properly insulated.

- **Electrician and plumber:** contact the electrician and plumber who, assisted by a worker, will have to "cut" the walls and the floor and then channel their pipes. Both technicians will have to prepare the installations according to the law and according to the project, using the appropriate materials, and trace their installations from the command point to the central plant. The electrician will have to discuss about how you want to equip and equip the house to understand the necessary power and adapt an authorized electrical panel, then making the related requests to the administration company. The plumber instead will ask how you want to install the home boiler (boiler) and will also discuss the location of the water safety keys. Both will propose ideal points of water and light in the most common points, according to their criterion, but here also the user will have to give his opinion according to his needs and the result will be a mix of requests, standards and advice based on the experience of other previous works. Also contact specialized technicians, for example that of air conditioners to have the desired machinery ready.

- **Carpenter, installer, tiler, plasterer, carpenter:** call these skilled workers to carry out work that cannot be damaged, even if you continue to work in the house. Barriers, stairs, ornaments, counter-ceilings, bathroom and kitchen tiles, floors can be made only if it is not a delicate surface that can be damaged, such as for example wood and similar surfaces: in this case it is expected that almost everyone has finished and poses, or alternatively poses and covers themselves to protect it, but at the risk of ruining it. Similarly, the first finishes and details can be made. There is always to keep in mind that if you choose a so-called floating floor, that is superimposed on the existing floor, this installation must be done before commissioning the doors because the height of the floor will obviously vary and consequently also the size of the new doors to be requested on assignment. Normally we tend to leave the change of doors and windows last (being able for safety reasons), so as not to run the risk of ruining new materials due to the great coming and going of people and especially the transport and assembly of new furniture or furniture. antique furniture that had been moved. The fixtures and doors and walls are then finished with the relative skirting boards or decorations, which have the function of protecting the materials and hiding any cutting or installation defects.

- **Painter:** normally he is the last to arrive and is in charge of fixing all the small defects and then covering them first with white, and then giving personality to the house with color. In theory, he should paint in white before there is the assembly of the new furniture and once mounted devote himself to color: this would facilitate the times and the task of the painter, but if it were not possible you can do everything later. What is advisable is not to immediately throw in the request for random colors: it is advisable to first have a "clean version" of the house and then proceed to color the walls or the specific areas, consistently with the furniture chosen and with the decorations and style of the house. It is up to the taste of the owner and who designed the house to direct the painter in the chromatic choices and in the areas where to intervene.

- **Furniture, lights, decorations:** lastly we find the fun, but not secondary, part of beautifying the home: many people often do it "by chance" by mixing styles, colors and materials that have no coherence and ruining at the last moment something that it was thought and that it had an important cost. Always consult an expert also in this part, because it can give you new ideas and above all it can make a nice normal house, turn into a great house with unique character and personality. It is clear that then, depending on whether it is a home or long-term rental or holiday home, the decoration criteria will be very different from each other.

- **Exterior of the house:** it is the only item that can be independent from the rest and can have a non-consequential value: that is, it can be reformed or not even later or in a different time space. According to the technical characteristics of the house, it is necessary to intervene on roofs, façades, gardens, entrances, accessory spaces, gates, possibly on installations such as garages and swimming pools. Clearly this type of intervention requires "a whole separate discussion" which is not part of the themes of this book, but has much more to do with architecture. However, it is good to keep in mind that it is different when we speak of a single house rather than an apartment building, because obviously in the first case all costs and interventions are the responsibility of a single owner, while in the second case it is the intervention of a community of owners who decide and intervene proportionally by bringing capital to the common parts: to know that the common parts are normally the responsibility of the communities (such as parking spaces, entrance, lift, inner court, roofs, general and centralized water, electricity and telecommunications systems and everything outside, including balconies unless they are private): the jurisdiction of the Community ends where private property begins, i.e. at the front door, always compatibly with compliance with laws and permits also for the reform of interiors.

HOME-STAGING

We have defined this practice as a "touch-up", a trick: in a certain sense it is a good definition because it evokes something magical, that is, something that "with little" offers substantial changes and an appearance completely different from the point of origin.

In reality this system of intervening on a house is much more complex and presupposes an art, an aesthetic sense, a capacity for functional organization, a study and the knowledge that a non-professional user hardly possesses, as normally his attention and is concentrated on the aesthetic result in an almost total way. First of all, we need to talk about the economic resources: there is no doubt that making an intervention on a property, whether it is to be completely renovated or to be retouched, can be more or less easy depending on the estimate drawn up. It is very easy to make an intervention when there is an unlimited budget: the best materials and the best furniture on the market would be bought and therefore already half of the work would be easily carried out. Often, however, it is necessary to live together and adapt with risky, if not insufficient, estimates and it is here where a professional in the sector can have an extra gear: we tend to think that he is an extra person to pay, but "who would not pay for a person who saves on materials and suppliers, offering his experience to have, in addition to a lower outlay, a better result?". A *home-staging* professional normally collaborates with a few different *teams* of trusted technicians with whom he repeats more jobs, and thanks to this he manages to have better prices, and due to his experience he knows where to buy certain materials at less price or where and how achieve the best discounts. Aside from being able to considerably reduce costs, it holds innovative skills and ideas that mixed with the investor's ideas can be brilliant and produce incredible results with houses that totally change appearance and unexpected solutions with obvious attention to the easy use and optimization of spaces and details. Needless to talk about the aesthetic result that can be obtained not only with the furniture, but also through the use of materials instead of others, the use of colors instead of others, the use of lights and the use of an aesthetic sense and practical that derives from experience and study and attention to detail. It is the most creative part of a house, which is why many investors think of skipping this step, having fun in the first person, using *do-it-yourself*, but often the result is monotonous, standardized or impractical because attention is paid to aesthetics. and not for use. A good *home-staging* professional can enhance a house and increase its value, or find solutions to limit some defects or totally upset it with little estimate to make it acquire a character or personality different from the one it held. In reality it could be compared to a stylist: we all like to dress each one in our own style, but this does not necessarily mean that we know how to dress well. If we talk about feeling comfortable then only personal criteria apply, but when we have to dress for an anniversary or a purpose there are criteria that often elude us. Like a fashion designer, the *home-staging* professional is the home stylist: therefore, depending on the destination-use of that investment, he will have to adapt functional and aesthetic spaces to optimize the use that the investor wants. make. Careful to a detail: furnishing a holiday home or furnishing a private home **is not the same thing**; there are absolutely different needs in terms of space, needs and functions of the same furniture even: we think of a wardrobe and just the dimensions without going into quality. For example, a tourist does not need more than a *two-door wardrobe* for two suitcases and a couple of weeks of holidays, while a resident probably has 2 wardrobes. They are not secondary details to think about later, but they are things to think about during the design phase, if we think for example of the case of built-in wardrobes or the size of a room, which suddenly could become very small, when we only remembered at the end that we you need an extra wardrobe. Aside from the equipment, there is also a difference in warmth or personality or style of the house on which to intervene, because it is always different to prepare an environment for someone who stays temporarily or for someone who must live there. The design, combined with lights and atmospheres must be coherent and follow certain criteria of balance, to give the desired result in terms of elegance rather of a rustic character, or of modernity rather than *vintage* character, or of intimacy rather of a *loft*-like room. This type of intervention can act on accessory objects, or change of furniture, or change of wall colors. We must seek a balance of style and harmony between colors and objects and spaces: needless to say that *do-it-yourself* in these cases can be harmful in results, similar to a collection of *junk*.

SCALAR INVESTMENTS TO RENT

It is quite obvious that more properties are administered in number, and more incomes can be organized and thus increase profits. It's called scaling a business: that is, when you can replicate a production model several times to get more revenue.

In the real estate sector, it is a game that is quite dangerous on the one hand because the capital invested is considerable, both for the purchase and for the taxes rather than for the renovations. It is true, however, that on the other hand, a correct real estate investment is also a fairly safe and solid asset because as much as it can lose value in the worst conditions, when it is well organized and well located, it never goes under certain standards and with time and market fluctuations it can recover value. It is certain that when making irreparable errors of inexperience, such as buying at crazy prices or out of location, then, returning from the investment becomes complicated. When you even buy a property by mistake that has clear and obvious neighborhood, structure or market problems, clearly things get even more complicated. This is why many buyers turn to renowned real estate agencies and often choose a trusted real estate agent. A homeowner is always convinced that his home is the best and will always try to sell it as a private individual, highlighting only its strengths. Buyers love to buy with real estate because they can understand the true value of a house, because they will want to see more than one (willingly or unwillingly) (even if they tried to hide alternatives from them, they would go and see them by themselves and they would lose contact with the customer, because they are not buying a shirt that you like in 5 minutes and you can decide with your eyes closed for fun!). If you think that in the modern sales system, buyers do not pay agency commissions, it is normal for them to choose a better service that also costs them nothing. For this reason many times, the cause of a slowdown in the sale of a property, to great surprise, is **the owner himself**, who is not a professional in the sector, cannot express the same arguments as a good agency, does not express the same trust to the buyer customer and hinders the work of the real estate agent with his resistances: often as professionals "it takes more to obtain the assignment of sale of an owner than to sell the house ". Also because, at times, it grants it however with off-market claims and therefore a mediation process must be implemented, before with the buyer, with him because he analyzes the market with responsibility and conscience and realizes the correct dynamics and numbers to reach the result of the sale. It is not always true that "whoever spends, spends better ", less in this field. Therefore, in order to optimize earnings, investment should be scaled down, which in this reality presupposes huge capital or an excellent relationship with banks (which in any case means having large capital deposited as collateral). If through this, through the other creative financing movements or through the recruitment of a group of investors, it is possible to multiply the investment and reproduce it in series, then you can think of differentiating the type of activity (medium and long term) or geographical locations, or types of houses (by size or intended use or style).

In this case, we would also protect ourselves from the changes in fashions and from economic fluctuations exactly as happens on the stock exchange when we diversify and scale an investment in shares on distinct markets with different products.

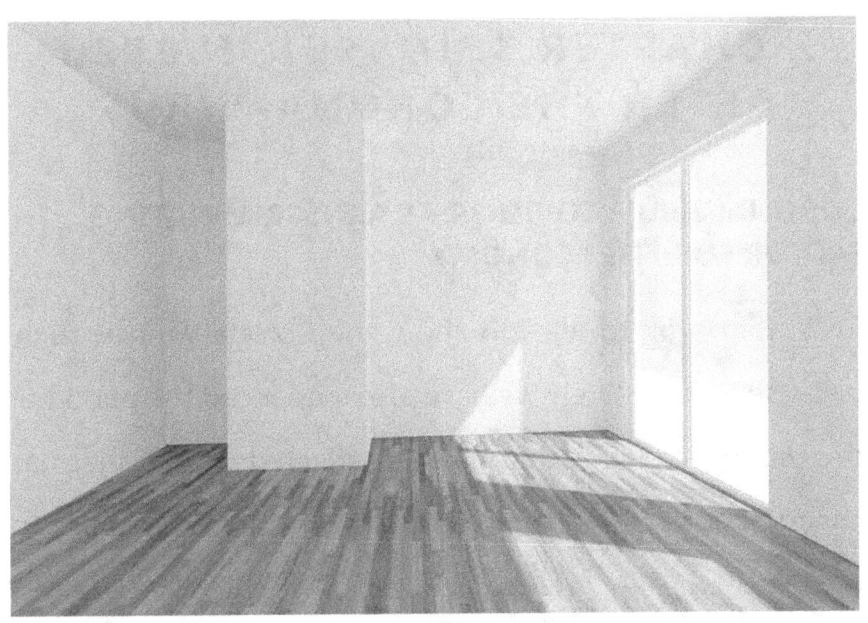

"There is a whole new market after the covid-19 "

CHAPTER 3: INVEST IN 2020 AFTER THE CORONA-VIRUS

CORONA-VIRUS: COVID-19 AS A DISCRIMINATING FACTOR FOR THE ECONOMY

I will not go on to tell you about the Corona-virus as such, because unfortunately we have all experienced the period of this world pandemic that has just affected us and that has changed our lives, forcing us to take refuge in the house to escape them, but irremediably blocking the system direct economic impact of several countries (indirectly affecting the entire world economy as a result). We all already know where it was born and how it spread, we know the numbers of victims and the limiting measures we had to take, but we don't know exactly the numbers of the economic damage yet: we may perhaps have a personal idea, which varies from company to company a company, according to what was invoiced in 2019 and will not be invoiced in 2020, but the consequences of all this will not be limited to 2020 alone and exactly it is difficult today to estimate how much it will affect the following years.

Do you wonder this consideration? Perhaps someone had deluded themselves that with a few months of isolation all this would pass and it could be cataloged as a bad memory to be forgotten as soon as possible. Unfortunately this will not be the case and even if they are only theories, I will try to explain them to you in the most practical way possible, through examples, so that everyone can ask their own questions. "Questions": yes, because no one is currently able to give absolute answers; you can only make assumptions.

What is certain is that nothing will be the same as before, because the contemporary world has found itself vulnerable to something that not even Bin Laden and his terrorist organization had come to do: in 2011, in fact, the terrorist acts had made the most supportive and united world, strengthened the desire to unite and collaborate to overcome what had been a vile attack. It was almost as if terrorism had been defeated, apart from that by the US military, by itself, as it brought about the union under the flag of the United Nations, with an unimaginable sense and desire for freedom and pro-positivity: the terrorists' followers had frightened, but they had certainly not blocked the world: the world instead blocked it covid-19 nine years later.

In fact, this bizarre virus, underestimated by all, has gone quite hidden for months, disguising itself with strange episodes classified then as simple "pneumonia" in the worst cases or spreading among the asymptomatic. He was not known, and therefore no one feared him, and at the beginning he positioned himself strategically, to then appear officially in China and later in Germany with the patient or European; but not officially he was already around the world, probably from the second half of 2019, sly, silent. Then when the "bubble" exploded and the numbers collapsed, this bizarre enemy was given name and surname, and then the fear began, above all because we discovered that we could not face it, neither from a medical point of view (no vaccine), nor were we ready with the facilities and numbers to deal with it from the point of view of the health emergency, with the various national systems *overloaded* in a few weeks. This time the enemy had hit his target: not only the direct victims, but all the consequences: *fear outside the front door*. To demonstrate the weakness of an entire nation, of many countries even. And above all to separate, since it was one of the few wars in which the peoples, after reaching stability, felt more divided than ever: the various nations did not react uniformly, but in drops, they implemented very policies different in timing and reactions. There was solidarity and it is true, but late and in most cases not very effective. People have reduced themselves to locking themselves up frightened (and not understanding) in their homes, without even having often embraced a family member. It was one of the few wars that divided "before, during and after", also because "loving each other in that moment hurt", that is, you had to separate and distance yourself to stay safe: any contact could have been risky. Months of this psychological and media massacre that will change the way we perceive life forever. Unfortunately, those who will surely constitute the most significant legacy will not be good intentions, easy to forget in a few months, but the economic and social consequences of the thing.

COVID-19 LETTER TO THE POSTERITY

I want to bring back a letter from an anonymous person, which was launched on the net, during the health crisis and which is very significant humanly; but it is also strategically so as to be able to understand what will happen in the months and years to come; in this letter the virus wrote to us in the first person just to give its version of the facts:

"Hi, I'm covid-19, many of you will know me more simply as Corona-virus; sorry for the short notice, but I am not given to let you know when I will arrive, in what form and in what strength I will present myself to you. Why am I here? Well, let's say why I was tired of seeing you regress rather than evolve, I was tired of seeing you continually ruin with your hands, I was tired of how you treat the planet, of how you relate to each other; I was tired of your abuses, of wars, of your interpersonal conflicts, of your prejudices; I was tired of your social envy, your greed, your hypocrisy, your selfishness; I was tired of the little time of the little time that you dedicate to yourself, to your families: I was tired of the little attention that you give too often to your children; I was tired of the importance you often give to superfluous things in spite of the essential ones; I was tired of your frantic and obsessive search for the most beautiful dress, the latest *smartphone* model, the most beautiful machine just to appear made; I was tired of your betrayals; I was tired of too much misinformation, of the little time you spend communicating among yourself. I was very tired of your constant complaints when you do nothing to improve your lives. I know, I'll be hard on you, maybe too much, but I don't look at anyone: I'm a virus. And the message I want to give is simple: **I wanted to highlight all the limits of the society in which you live,** so that you can eliminate them; I wanted to stop everything so that you understand from now on, that the only thing that matters, to which you will have to direct all your energies from now on is simply "life"; yours and that of your children, and what is strictly necessary to protect, pamper and share it. I wanted you as much as possible locked up and isolated in your homes, away from your parents, your grandparents, your children or grandchildren, because you understand how important a hug, human contact, dialogue, a handshake, a walk in the centre, a dinner in some restaurant or a run in the open air park: everything must start from these gestures. You are all the same! Make no distinction between you. I am passing through, but the feelings of closeness and collaboration that I have tried to create among you in a very short time will have to last forever. Live your lives as simply as possible: walk slowly, breathe, do good. Enjoy nature, do what satisfies you most and create the conditions for not having to depend on anything anymore. When you celebrate, I will have just left, but remember not to try to be better people only in my presence. Farewell".

This letter is very beautiful, and full of meanings and teachings: personally the only thing I do not share is the passage where he says that this experience has united us, because in the previous paragraph I just stated the opposite, and also because it would be a "vision or hope", but in reality we have already seen in the facts that this is not the case. Perhaps the desire and purpose we have is to be closer, closer, but let's stop dreaming and open our eyes, because unfortunately after all this people will also have good feelings, but frankly they will be afraid.

And the economy will suffer absolutely from this, with immediate financial and indirect direct effects in the coming years, changing the social perception and habits of people and therefore of investors.

The effort that we will therefore make in this part of our path is to try to hypothesize what the post-covid-19 investment scenarios could be both as regards the residential real estate field, and as regards the "commercial", on the basis of the experience lived in the previous economic crises and on the basis of the first market indications of which we have perception.

HOW THE REAL ESTATE MARKET CHANGES FROM 2020 ONWARDS

At the end of 2019 I was going to record my recurring videos of updates on the situation of the real estate market in my area of competence, and well in advance I highlighted how much the forecasts of the following year would have been clearly alarming, predicting and anticipating a real estate crisis in the final 2020: probably, I was wrong, but only because I was optimistic, I could not know of the virus that inexorably did nothing but anticipate the steps that would have occurred anyway for other reasons: the aforementioned Brexit, tour operator crisis, new Middle East limelight and inflation of holiday homes. I therefore expected the approach of an economic crisis (and of a real estate reflex) which would lead to the devaluation of the properties within a year, and *firstly* those less positioned or distinct. How well we all understand by now, this process is already underway and everything is going very quickly. The peculiarity of this crisis is that it will have gone from a final of the year 2019, with very high prices to a beginning of 2020 with prices in sharp fall: all in the space of a few months and without notice. This in the residential field, where however there will be differences for very unique properties or for particularly interesting areas; it will probably be a catastrophe for commercial activities, of which a good part already had to make drastic decisions, such as "closing down" or selling, perhaps at a very devalued price, in a hurry. In the future, there will probably be a kind of **natural selection**, where those who do not have a certain professionalism or economic strength are destined to disappear from the market.

In a sense, not all evils come to harm because this will, in the long run, lead to greater average quality and less "inflation", but during this change there is always someone worthy who unfortunately cannot "stand up. "(And someone who is less deserving than with artifices or economic solidity resists and therefore queues up to the best). The important issue will therefore soon be that of liquidity. How is this reflected on investments? The most obvious consequence is the lowering of prices on sales, but there is also to be taken into account that prices also go down because there are fewer people with the opportunity to buy. In reality, the market will return to being a market of "buyers" (that is, where the buyer is holding the negotiations), because there are already many investors who were organizing and not moving, waiting for the favourable market swing to buy. as soon as the prices were more accessible.

In recent years, in fact, there had been a fairly widespread arrogance on the part of the owners in setting the values of their properties, and the *good investor* had stopped buying, "letting buy" only private individuals, who had personal interests, rather than contingent needs, and they certainly could not wait years for a business cycle to change. So to think that there are no buyers is wrong, but now **the type of buyer will change**: be careful, however, not to be fooled by the "myth of the investor". Many times we have heard opinions of sellers who defined their properties or businesses as "perfect for an investor", often supported only by their personal desire or interest to believe in this thing.

Investor does not mean "dumb". Quite the opposite! The veteran investor, for example, is the exact antipode of the owner from the front, that is to say, through his communication, that "everything is less, really, than the value that is being attributed to it". So on the one hand the owner has a tendency to swell; on the other, the aggressive investor has a tendency to demonstrate that it is worth much less in the market.

How can owners ever hope in vain for investors as saviors of the homeland? The reality is that they are investment professionals and are not used to buying off the market.

"Sometimes I have been offered marketing assignments, for ancient buildings, at a price that we define in this example as 100. The objective that according to the owner I should have found was "an investor", *because a private individual could not afford that outlay*": the first thing you do in these cases, look on the agenda for the first 5 numbers of the most important investors in the city and start calling. Unfortunately, often the answer is "Thanks, but I'm not interested, because I'm selling "the new one at 110", and therefore it costs too much. In fact, I would buy what you offer me, in a price between 50-60 because maybe it is worth

70. So considering all the expenses, at this price you propose is uneconomical". *It is quite obvious that I refuse regardless of assignments of this type*, just after having informed the owner of responses of this type (and having seen that his reaction is absurd: "then let's try to lower it to 95". "But if it is 70?!"). I hope it is quite clear that for this type of owner, **the investor will never be a resource,** just as this property will never be purchased by an investor (and probably under these conditions not even by a private individual), because it is out of the market.

So I'm painting a very problematic scenario, where there will be an absolute need for a change of *mind-set* by the owners and responsibility by the buyers: the former will necessarily have to adapt to the market, unless they decide and can afford to wait a new economic cycle in a few years, and the latter will not have to "pull the rope too much" and present absurd offers. From the balance of the two positions, the real estate system will return to turn and produce, and surprisingly it could be one of the first to recover, at least in the residential area in certain geographic areas. Everything therefore depends on the *mind-set* and the balance between supply and demand: the faster the adaptation to the new market, the faster the transactions will return.

SOCIAL AND ECONOMIC CHANGES

If it is true that therefore the paralysis of the real estate system is not expected, but simply a change, on the other hand, a radical change in the uses and customs of people and the consequent economic shift of wealth by sectors is very certain.

As we learned in the letter written by covid-19, this experience will change certain systems and ways of thinking, and above all it will concern entrepreneurship and the way of thinking about corporate life. Perhaps the real function of the virus, in the end, will be to really bring us into the XXI century, because until now everything had remained exactly the same as the XX century, with a slow and inexorable expiration of products and service in general.

Is this the occasion for a real economic-industrial revolution?
The first effects of this experience have been seen in commerce and services. Having been the first activities blocked by the restrictive decrees, they closed the physical store and organized or strengthened an existing *online trade*. Obviously, bars, for example, cannot prepare us a *cocktail online,* nor offer us aggregation and fun; but apart from these cases, let's think about the marketing of clothes,

housewares, products in general, and food products themselves (many people have started to request more supermarket home service for fear of going out to buy firsthand): previously only a small niche used these *online services* in this sense, but with limited confinement, for months, they have become more and more accustomed to searching the internet for a product and to request it for shipping. In this sense, it is plausible to think that companies of this type, for the future, will further strengthen this branch, and this could also change the logic of the stores, which have always worked until yesterday. It is quite obvious and obvious that there will therefore be many changes from an organizational and social point of view, because people will get used to different things to meet their needs, and of this the market will have absolutely everything in mind. In the real estate market, therefore, the valuations will change, certainly also the strategies in the commercial field, which will determine new rules: now more than ever it will be necessary to look to the future, because another type of game is played.

RESIDENTIAL MARKET: WHAT CHANGES

The property has always had a fairly important and clear intrinsic value since the earliest times. Remember in the *old West*, when colonies and colonies of people went in search of luck. I am not talking about speculative and random search for gold, but about a more solid and secure form of investment or "land". This example means how ephemeral certain and even risky investments are, in spite of others who are absolutely always functional and with low probability of risk: "**a house is always a house,** it is worth a lot or it loses value, it will always be worth something", and by holding the property it can be used for different uses:

- PERSONAL USE: we take into account that everyone needs a home, **used to reside and live.** The house can be "owned" or "long term rent".

An interesting assessment to make is that paradoxically we could say that in Europe, or in the United States, "there are more houses than families": if we do not take into account preferential and other discriminating and variable areas and we only look at cold numbers, there would be no need for real estate or real estate, since everyone has more than one roof available. Yet houses are still being manufactured and marketed! The main point is that for work, family, social or economic needs *the circumstances in life change* and therefore a circle is set in motion for which people move continuously from one property to another according to circumstances ": to this point the need becomes predominant and it can be safely said that "**everyone needs a house potentially**": this is the principle that moves the real estate world, born to solve the needs of people who constantly need a change.

In this case, the scenario will remain almost constant even today, because everyone will continue to need "a roof"; however, there may be a redistribution following covid-19.

Many people, who previously had commitments or debts or economic problems, it is easy to assume that they have worsened their situation: it is reasonable to think that if they are owners, they are thinking of selling, then renting a house and attributing it to their first residence. Similarly, those who were renting and had problems could think of moving to areas or to a cheaper property. In both cases there will be wills and predispositions to real estate type "movements".

- PROFITABLE USE: following the reasoning above, the owners, who can instead afford to count with significant savings and liquidity, taking advantage of the opportunities of the moment, have acquired and are acquiring more than one property and if sometimes this is used as second residence (for pleasure) or to carry out its commercial or industrial activity, in other cases the purpose is to invest to rent to a third party. In the case of the lease, therefore, we can say that the property was purchased in order to produce capital. These capitals would be "income from *long, medium or short-term* leases depending on the policies adopted by the owner. By defining **the long term as "stable typology"**, the medium term as an "innovation", interesting to monitor, and the short term as "speculative" and following trends, we can assume that in the post Corona-virus it will continue and will be recommended "l "long-term rent", to compensate for the needs of personal use, as it has always been in every age and in every crisis; I would like to put a question mark on "medium-term" or seasonal rental, because it will also and above all follow migration logics and work needs, which are still not well defined after the crisis; in any case, I would venture to advise, because it is at least certain that it is a type of investment with low competition, and therefore potentially profitable. Instead, I would give for short term or at least inflated and intended for a small group of strong investors, the rent of "short term" or for tourism. Few really strong and organized, with first-order positions will remain in the market, but the vast majority and above all or the owners of "common and anonymous" properties, are destined to sell or convert this business model to another, because it was in decline much earlier of covid-19: now all this will lead inexorably to the breakdown of the toy, at least on a large scale: do you think it is a catastrophic forecast? Let's try to think of the property defined as "for personal use", which has always endured over time: the secret of this durability is that it is **necessary**. Is the "holiday home" necessary? Or is it rather a superfluous good?

In 2020, the direct losses of the economic crisis will be calculated in a figure higher than 30%, because there has been a "general stop" and people have been unable to move or go to work. Everyone is super convinced that after this period of "imposed chastity", there will come a period of wicked expenses in travel and parties, to compensate for the shortcomings that have suffered in the previous period. They are wrong: they are not dealing with the new habits that people have developed, and with the fear of what has happened or what may still happen. In a nutshell, although there will have been a huge Saturday of exaggerated parties and celebrations, the rest of the weekends will never be similar to before, at least in a short period, despite all the intention and desire for freedom. Unconsciously people will remain conditioned and divided for a long time, suspended between "memory and desire to leave", and this will generate uncertainty. Equity markets will be very cautious: this means that so will investors in the various fields; unless particularly advantageous occasions occur, these will not move, while they will be very fast if a product is placed on the market that is absolutely in line with the correct and current value. To return then to the short-term lease talk, how many investors do you think will leave that market and how many will want to enter it instead? Starting from the point of view that, even before, there was absolute saturation of that type of market, it is quite obvious to think that with a *fractional demand* and now super reduced by events, this business model is no longer intended for anyone as until a few years ago. In fact, after a first binge, people will not be as inclined to move and to dedicate their savings to holidays as previously, because they have discovered that they have other needs and priorities. We do not neglect that, since not being able to work, both entrepreneurs and employees will have fewer resources available, and therefore less tourism circulation is expected than in previous years. Some inexperienced investors may object by saying that given the scenario "not all tourists will want to go to an expensive hotel" and will choose to fall back on *his "home in a shared house, perhaps with common services, and located not in the main position"*: I will reply by stating that an investor must have a 360-degree global vision and not only look at his own personal need: tourism is not only the stay, but also travel and food costs (for an independent person it is even the failure gain during your absence from work). We cannot underestimate the general context of recession and think that it does not touch the "holiday homes". Furthermore, we could also add that a "scalar model of holiday homes", for example that of large companies that rent large tourist complexes or tour operators that rent entire hotels (or part of them at advantageous prices), can offer more services at this point. much more competitive prices than before, because they will want to recover their market share. To compete with those who have the greatest economic means, quality and position, could really be something absolutely senseless. For this reason, I personally feel absolutely advised against the market entry of a beginner investor in this field, in this historical moment, because this game has become only for a few expert players.

- NO USE: I will surprise you by talking about this category because it is very interesting. "Who tells you that all properties serve some function?". They could only exist as a result of unplanned circumstances and be completely superfluous or even annoying (if we think that they must be maintained by paying taxes and maintenance to own them, without perhaps making use of them). We talk about wrong investments for example, never finished or unfinished, which therefore are not even in a condition to be rented, or we think of the inherited properties: the covid-19 or life in general, leave traces in 2020 of many deaths; many of these people were owners and therefore their heirs could either be new owners (and move from the condition of rent to that of having a first home) or they could simply inherit properties in unexpected form of which they do not objectively know what to do with them. These properties will be real **market opportunities**, in many cases because, once the emotional barrier has been overcome, if careful commercial evaluations are made, there will be *a good sales motivation* and therefore market-compliant prices: in these conditions, many potential investors will want to win them for personal or investment purposes. It is difficult, unfortunately even if sometimes it happens, to think that good properties remain unused to ruin inexorably over time: a wise owner will have to think how to use that capital before it devalues, because time deteriorates it without remedy.

COMMERCIAL MARKET: WHAT CHANGES

In this field, total uncertainty reigns, because the extent of what has happened is still to be measured. We have previously mentioned a sort of natural selection, **where the best or those with the most financial resources will survive**, and also a sort of change in the structuring of certain points of sale and consequently of type of property: if, for example, it took hold scale the selection and automated delivery of *supermarket shopping*, it is reasonable to think that small shops would suffer the latest lethal blow, and that food companies would dive into huge warehouses and warehouses, organizing *Amazon*-style deliveries, instead of aiming to manage expensive stores located in strategic places.

Natural selection and change of concept are in progress, therefore the effects of these changes cannot yet be predicted. However, we have also mentioned an old and expensive sector, which however cannot be expressed with today's technologies and cannot be performed in virtual form, because it has to do with the aggregation and production of "something done at the moment"; if you think about it, it is really the only thing that cannot have a corresponding virtual version. In fact, even if it is not the same, in extreme conditions you can see a football game virtually, or order any product and service, or make meetings and have friends and even a virtual girlfriend: but you will never "go to the bar virtually ". The *food & beverage* sector is not a type of trade that can be replicated in virtual form. Certainly therefore, if on the one hand the classic shop risks disappearing due to the social changes or habits that people, restaurants, bars and hotels would assume, as "sellers of aggregation and emotions" and a product that can only be used in a three-dimensional way "Live", they will continue their existence, albeit undergoing an important inflection of the numbers for the reasons already explained. However, there will also be an important exchange of sellers here who, due to the change in customer habits or the accounts which are no longer favorable, will decide to sell, creating important market opportunities, in positions or situations that until some time ago were unthinkable. The real "sharks" (expert investors), should be ready now with their capital to position themselves and take advantage of these market opportunities.

But what is the identikit of this type of investor?

It is absolutely a very expert and abundant profile, because the first thing that will be clear is that it will not begin to earn in the short term, but his is an investment over time: **he is only buying a good position at an advantageous price**, but it is very probable that if he wants to assemble an activity today, he will have difficulties like everyone else, unless he again resorts to economic resources to build and position an activity as *market leader*. The beginner investor then? Someone from this other group will surely move equally, even in unfavorable conditions, and will probably burn especially if they do not have specific skills in the business and economic reserves to deal with times of depression. All economic cycles offer market opportunities: the theme is "knowing how to read the score in advance" and move accordingly.

AND IF TOMORROW THERE WAS A NEW "CROWN-VIRUS"?

We are describing scenarios and trying to make sense of assumptions, but if on the one hand it is legitimate to think that in a reasonable period we return to normal (or better said, we find a new balance and a new reality), on the other part it is legitimate to ask, if tomorrow a *new invisible enemy*, cannot arrive from some distant land, and force us to start over again with the same problems encountered with this accident, or even with other new problems. To answer this we must look at history: what happened after the great wars or the great international financial and economic depressions.

As entrepreneurs, we cannot stop (and we never stopped at any time in history), in spite of the events, we have always adapted and it is normal to think that in terms of investments, after a first prudential period, we return to express a normal and physiological volume, which allows the economy to return to function properly. If ever the is tendentious in another sense: "It is not that I start investing, and in 10 years I am in full bacteriological war that in fact puts my investment on the ropes? (and therefore it was better not to invest)". Nobody is known about the development of the future, but it is obviously an eventuality that could return to take place and it must be taken into account. But we must also use some available tools such as history and statistics to see that in one hundred years it is "only" the second pandemic that has occurred, and that if we really want to talk about catastrophes, surely the Second World War was it was another kind of event, much more harmful in every sense. A hypothetical nuclear war, for example, would be even more so, and in that case perhaps the economic problem would be only the bottom of a long list. If you think conditioned by fear of what may possibly happen in the future, it is quite obvious that the whole system becomes paralyzed and that no one undertakes any activity. But an entrepreneur, by definition, is a person who moves, who uses resources and means, to organize them for a purpose. To undertake means "always to risk", also and the system of investing in the most profitable way with the least possible risk is continuously sought. Taking all the necessary steps, is it statistically more plausible that one catastrophe follows another or that a beginner investor makes an investment wrong? There are wrong investments in the world every 20 seconds, that is, people who in a reckless way misuse the means at their disposal and instead of producing benefits, they produce losses. Investment will not decrease as a result of this crisis, but will simply change as we have already analyzed. Should something similar happen in the future, one thing is certain: it is hoped that on the basis of this experience, everyone will be more prepared next time and know what to do, because the great victory of this phenomenon has been *to catch everyone by surprise* and unprepared: no one knew absolutely "what to do", *from small to large up to the heads of State*. The difficulty and the economic crisis also derive from a difficult ability to react to something that was unpublished and which forced everyone to behave and defend themselves even in an unprecedented way. Should it happen again, the hope for the institutions is that they are prepared and remember the teachings of this crisis, and for people who do not let themselves be beaten down because **"it's in times of crisis that great stories and great opportunities "**. Surely all this has destabilized us, demobilizing us from a certain *comfort zone*, which after 1945 had always been fairly regular in its various oscillations. But sometimes getting out of the *comfort zone* allows you to move forward and grow and there will certainly be investors and entrepreneurs *capable of growing and growing* in the coming years. Growth is something inherent and natural in man. Evolution has shown that, despite the mistakes made and the great disasters, it has always managed to move forward. It would be surprising if there was a regression after all this: there may be a crisis, a decline, but we will not go back to the "age of stone", unless the irremediable really happens and the prophecy of famous science fiction film "the planet of the apes": it is a classic, but for those who do not know it "it is the story of man's regression to an almost primitive state after a nuclear war or in any case a catastrophic scenario: few species animals had survived and the evolutions and values in the field had changed, so much so that the men, deprived of their technology, had remained firm in a practically medieval condition, and the apes had evolved enough to reach and almost surpass man. Hollywood's film ends with the protagonist, who, escaping the monkeys' clutches, goes in desperate search for his *lost identity* and the memories he had lost: he ends up finding himself in the *old world* he knew, beyond the forbidden area, where, however, 'finds nothing but rubble and desolation; understands and recalls that it was once part of a large human race, which is now mediocre and has lost everything. End the film with the protagonist on his knees and defeated".

This science fiction scenario, the result of a hypothetical nuclear or bacteriological conflict, for the moment let's leave it to cinema and science fiction.

In the world we know, the economic system will recover, reshaping itself with new rules and balances over time. **The beginner investor will have to learn to move between the lines and adapt especially to the changes**: I would say that this will be the best feature he must have; before flexibility was very important, but now it will become fundamental. Flexibility and adaptability, as fundamental characteristics in the field of residential and commercial investments. On the other hand, *the leading companies in the sector* have traced the example and the road, even during the covid-19 crisis: let's think of those who had to close their productions, because the products were not basic necessities "; how many (open or not) have seen their production decrease directly or indirectly? But let's think about how they reacted, making the example of the most renowned fashion and textile companies for example: the world was not prepared for the Corona-virus and there was absolute absence or insufficiency of the famous *masks*. many textile industrialists, in the impossibility of continuing with a normal production of their products, they have converted their offer into the production of this article (or related articles such as clothing and gloves), resulting productive also in this period of time and perhaps in the future, having possibly paved the way as pioneers for new products and lines, given the awareness that will derive for everyone, following this experience. It is a very fitting example of *flexibility* and is one of the most important things in a period of change.

My main advice for a beginner investor is therefore not to lose heart, even if now he is forced to start in economic conditions deemed unfavorable, because they could open up new opportunities compared to the past, and it is said that we cannot take advantage of time to apply a forward-looking policy and implement a long-term winning strategy.

"The important thing is not how and when you fall, because it is to be taken for granted in an entrepreneurial path that this happens ", but it is essential to see how you get up! Above all, then it must be said that "who has fallen and has risen has acquired additional experience and maturity compared to a beginner ", therefore it is totally within the logic of natural and physiological growth. This is why you should not be afraid of investing, and you must plan your business project in detail and firmly believe in your ideas, because when something is set up correctly, personal and professional qualities emerge in the long run.

On the other hand, when a business is based on improvisation, lack of professionalism, short-term or very risky policies, the consequences can be devastating in any time or market condition: therefore the novice investor who will use a *do-it-yourself* policy, if he has the means, the time and the reserves to "make his own bones", prepare to pay (out of his own pocket) a very expensive training, based on errors and learning from them (what is called the typical learning "Based on poles in the face"), If on the contrary you are looking for a safer way, take care of assembled sensible projects and rely on sector professionals, from whom you can learn the secrets and from whom you receive assistance.

On the other hand, **investing is an art** that is learned, like any area of life and business, with time experience and the right teachers, and net of the uncontrollable variable that we call luck, it is absolutely not something accessible to everyone without distinction and that can be left to chance.

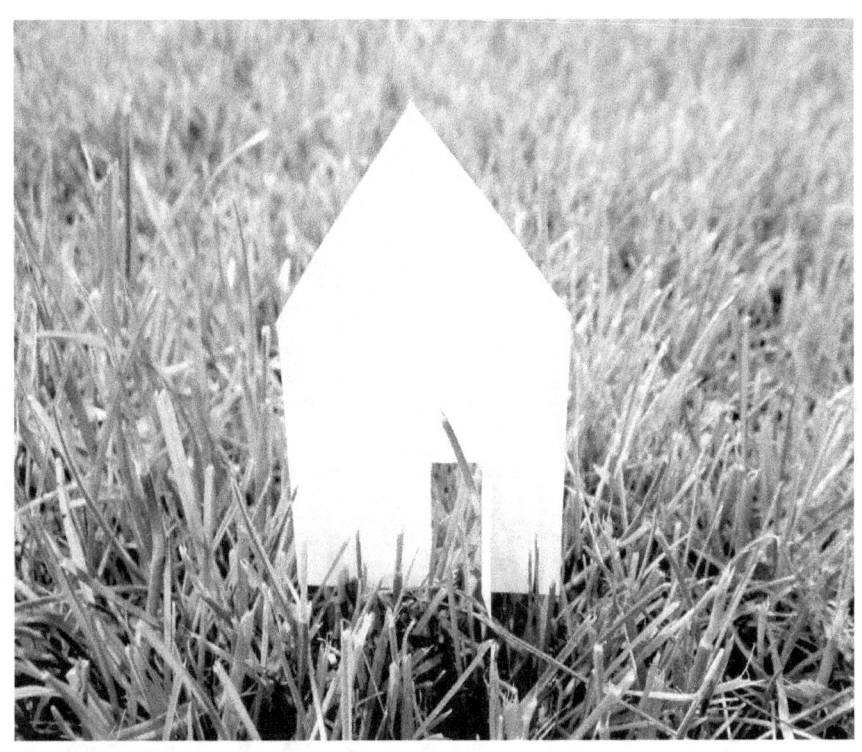

"Beautiful houses have a cost and are paid, but in the end they are always worth"

CHAPTER 4: THE RANKING AND IDENTIKIT OF THE BEST FORMS OF INVESTMENT PROPERTIES

Here we will make a list of the typology of the most attractive houses, also reinforced by some visual examples. Not all properties are in fact the same and also differ structurally in some very peculiar and important characteristics, regardless of the furnishings or everything they have inside them. Instead, they stand out for their architectural or location characteristics which are not modified and which determine their status as "different"; even "privileged", because it probably has unique characteristics that differentiate it and it is not so easy to find a similar product on the market. Let's think for example of a large city: we all know perfectly well that it is commonly very difficult to park, so parking spaces have great commercial value. It is therefore obvious, by reasoning applied, that properties with "parking space" have a significant added value, which is not only the value in itself of the garage, but rather **an additional value of higher "satisfaction and evaluation",** which a potential customer can attribute it. In this specific case, for example, there is a very important rule: never sell the separate garage, and in any case never sell it before the house: this is because the property would lose popularity, and will have less potential public ready to buy it. So it is reasonable to think that a house with a garage in the city has a higher price than another that does not have it available; in reality the potential value will still be much higher! Another bad news for all investors who had bought *holiday homes* (normally snubbing the garage theme because they thought that for a tourist it is not so important). Now that this type of investment will have to convert, play strength, towards longer periods, surely these properties will have one less weapon (therefore less value), because it is clear that those who live for a long period in a city have very different needs and could see "the garage theme" as very important, like the "elevator theme", for example, for which the same consideration applies.

So what are the most interesting and sought after properties from a real estate point of view?

Taking for granted that in 2020 we are all used to conveniences and therefore we like beautiful things, one of the common features that must have a good investment today, must be **the essential presence of the lift**: those who have the availability to invest absolutely want it, because he knows that the house has a higher value, and whoever engages in a mortgage also definitely wants it, because "already having to pay a fee every month for many years, he usually works for something of a certain value". Contrary to popular belief, young people are increasingly spoiled and if they come to buy they only want beautiful things! Older people for obvious reasons tend to avoid properties that do not have them.

So all the houses without a lift that are still being sold?

In the past few years, with the boom in holiday homes, people bought without thinking much about the lift-garage theme, because they wanted to buy the cheapest property on the market, prepare it and rent it to a typical tourist, who probably "was only a week away and he would not have complained too much for the absence of a lift and garage": in doing so he would save approximately 40-50000 euros, for example, that is "the added cost of an apartment in the same area, which is equipped with these characteristics".

In a market of madness, even this bad habit was fine, but how much will these properties be worth in a couple of years, with all the changes "on the doorstep" that we have already analysed? Not all properties have the same value, and buying well means first not to make any evaluation errors, especially in the architecture and location phase because they are two absolutely non-modifiable factors and therefore errors that are difficult to correct.

The most attractive properties, which will be destined for rent, are very similar to the best properties sought for use as a *first home*, and therefore must be selected according to medium-high quality criteria and with long-term logic. The typologies of *preferred properties* therefore coincide and are:

1) **CITIZEN PENTHOUSES:** they have always been one of the properties with exclusive character given the common feature of being the top floor and perhaps allowing views, apart from a brightness and independence different from a normal apartment. It is quite common that they also have exclusive spaces, such as an outside terrace for example. Always in the centre of large cities where there are only large buildings and there are no spaces to find single-family houses, they represent a *status symbol,* among the most sought after properties. Normally if they have a terrace with a view, the penthouses (obviously with a tweak on the economic evaluation) whose building does not have a lift or a parking space, are indiscriminately valid, for this reason they are exclusive and difficult to find on the market. For the rental topic, it is quite obvious that this type of property allows a higher tenant to be requested from a tenant, compared to a common apartment.

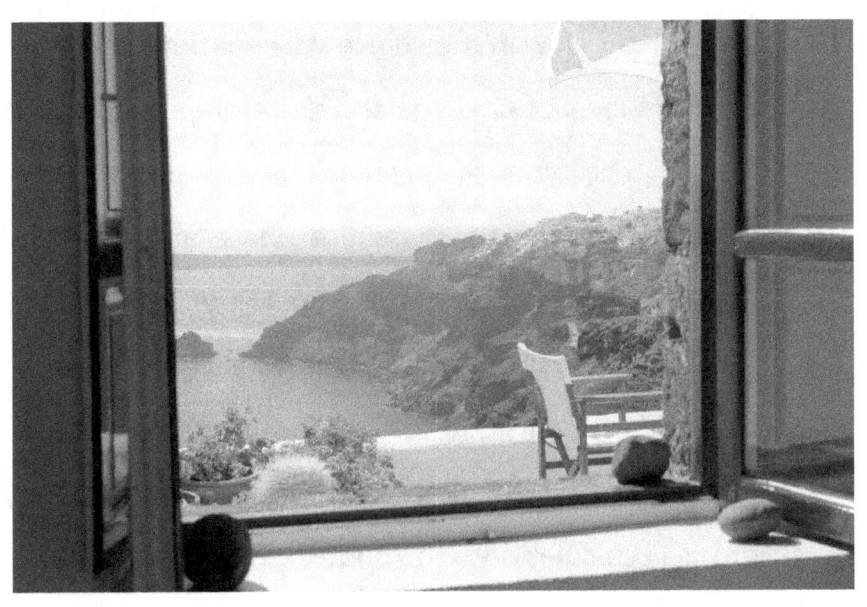

2) **HOUSE - APARTMENT WITH VIEWS:** there is an entire *elite* market where there are people willing to buy or rent houses in privileged positions, be these for example a sea view, a panoramic mountain view or an open air view in the centre. All situations that have a certain level of privilege and therefore are not easily found: this type of property is notoriously very expensive during the purchase phase and therefore for this reason, before thinking about making this type of investment to rent, you must have the very clear ideas: it will be necessary to set *ad hoc* terms for a very particular market and of course to make very precise calculations to understand what type of income a house of this type can generate and at what rental prices.

3) **CHALET PRIVILEGED AREA:** as a result of what has been said just now, if in the city centre by chance there is an independent house or chalet, it is certainly "rare goods". This type of house is more common to find outside the city, where the spaces are not "upwards", but develop by extension. On the outskirts or in the areas surrounding a city, there is often a residential area of terraced houses or chalet houses. It is quite clear that their value certainly varies with respect to size and shape, but also and above all based on location. "The "gold nugget" is often found far from other stones". On the subject of rents, being very expensive properties, there are not many used for this use: therefore generally there is a great demand to rent this type of houses, due to the presence of a scarce offer.

4) LARGE CITIZEN APARTMENT WITH GARAGE: it is the classic family apartment in the city, and therefore intended for the *evergreen* use of long-term rent. Precisely the definition of "family" refers to the need of families that this type of houses has essential characteristics, such as a lift and garage. Other welcome but accessory features are a good size and maybe the possibility of having a large living room and more bathrooms. Obviously, they are expected to have several bedrooms, possibly of a good size and with "facing" as much as possible from the outside. If by chance they are corner apartments, having multiple windows, they normally have greater value because they are more attractive and requested.

5) LARGE CITIZEN APARTMENT WITH TERRACE: we begin to define the difference between terrace and balcony: the terrace is a relatively large space, where furniture can be placed and an open air space can be used; often it is covered or closed, partially or completely, with wooden or aluminium structures, but in any case it does not lose its essence of detached, luminous and ample space, retaining large windows. The balcony, on the other hand, I would define it as a "view", that is a relatively smaller space where you can look out, to look at a view or to "smoke the classic cigarette". It is quite clear which is the most important option economically, even if we have to register great interests for houses "with simple balconies" towards others who do not even have this possibility. In fact, in large cities, depending on urban planning regulations, it should be borne in mind that houses of this type are worth even more and are "rare goods", given the many urban restrictions that sometimes prohibit the design with balconies, limiting it to only top floors (but the costs of an attic we have already said that they can be prohibitive for most investors):

for this reason apartments, even dated, but well located, with a nice terrace or balcony, are real "gold mines", because, regardless of their state inside, (thinking of the interior, they can be restructured to the investor's taste), the type with balcony is highly sought after because it is very rare to find in general.

6) WELL LOCATED MEDIUM CITIZEN APARTMENT:

when it is said that a property is like "a bank check" ... If well positioned and free from defects, this type of house is always fine, it has relatively low costs to buy and you always rent. It must not be too small and must have a separate bedroom. If it does not have this separation, it is defined as a *"studio apartment"*, that is a small "apartment", where the only room separated from the rest is the bathroom. The importance of having a bedroom separate from the rest remains clear, because above all in this example we note how much the choice of one or the other situation discriminates against the possible recipient of the rent: the studios can appeal to a *single* for the ease of maintenance they have and why maybe the lifestyle is in line with spending time outside the home. They may also appeal to students or people who move temporarily for work; but if you notice all the conditions mentioned are "provisional" and therefore will generate a type of "passing through" clientele. An apartment, with one or two bedrooms, is instead a clearly more expensive, but also more stable investment, intended for a type of tenant who stays longer over time.

7) CITIZEN APARTMENT WITH POOL OR OTHER BENEFITS: always intended for a particular public, even apartments with swimming pool or gym, gardens or other *benefits* are not too common, where there is always a sense of exclusivity, even if often these areas are common use. To be noted that the purchase costs normally do not vary normally, but the management costs absolutely vary, because having to administer the common areas of the condominium, obviously at the end of the month the owner must pay his own share destined for this type of expenses. Of course, this factor is reflected in the rental price for a possible tenant, who will still be the user of these *options.*

8) **"BATTLE" CITIZEN APARTMENT:** similarly to the existence of an *elite* market, there is a market of "tenants with few resources", who can afford to pay only low rents. In this case it is normal to understand that they do not generally have many structural or location needs. The discriminant of this type of property is the budget, so it is reasonable to think that there are investors interested in "buying low cost properties to rent them low cost" to this tenant profile: here for example all the property "without garage and without elevator", because clearly those who have less economic means also have more ability to adapt and are aware that they are paying a reduced price with minimal service.

9) OF SUBURBS: there is not only the city arket, but there is a whole market of *urban properties* in the suburbs, or in the hamlets, which have an important value: especially in the neighboring areas of the city, because who does not want to live in an apartment building, or want and need to live in a larger space, find your ideal location. These properties stand out and totally overturn the concepts expressed so far, because they work exactly the opposite for what their assessment is: in the suburbs there are more spaces and it is assumed that the price per square meter normally drops. So there is a tendency to find "the same price for a city apartment of 100 meters, and for a suburban chalet of 200 meters". In the suburbs, therefore, the value of the apartment located in an apartment building falls, with respect to the city, because it is more frequent to find real houses, even for rent. Normally the suburban house has a garage and a terrace, and indeed, where these characteristics do not exist, we can speak of lowering the potential value. What is very important and often determines the true property value of this type is the location and ease of road connections, and the privileged position (or not), with panoramic views or discreet surroundings.

11) **COUNTRY HOUSES WITH LAND:** "you do not understand how much demand there is for "country houses", until you start marketing the sale". In a nutshell everyone likes them, but it is an equally difficult type to place paradoxically, because they often have problems in documents or relations with the neighborhood or limitations related to the "intended use". In fact, a lot of interest is often connected to the intention, not only to cultivate the land (which is the natural use where there is often a fairly soft legislation), but the most common ambition to use them for the most disparate activities, from breeding a recreational park, from farm to hotel. In many cases, however, the law is limiting in this sense, and therefore, before venturing into such a purchase, it is good to be well informed of the activities allowed or not. In any case, for a canonical long-term rent there is normally no type of problem, and the same applies to the rent of the land for agricultural purposes, net of the stakes imposed by the individual municipalities.

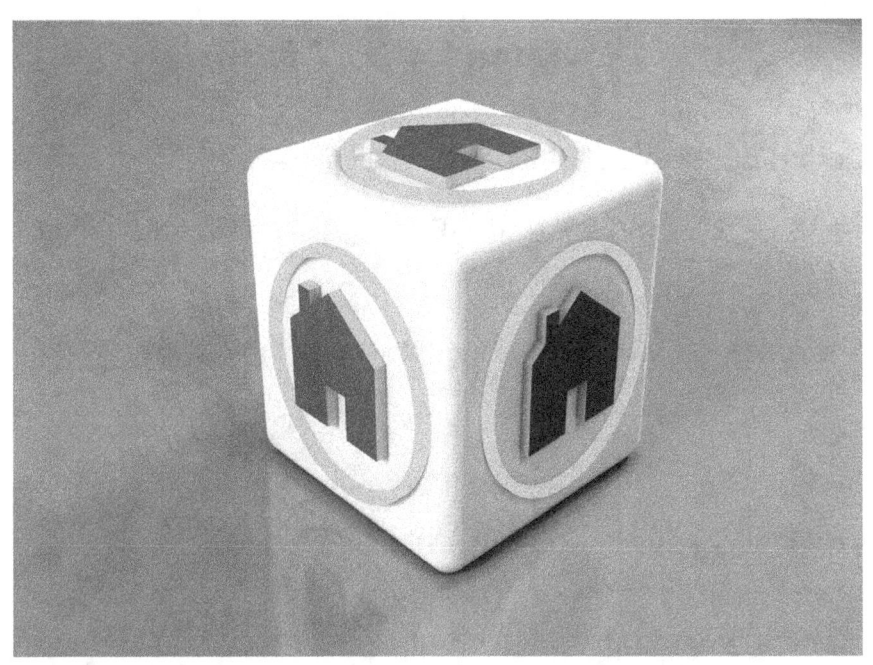

"...never think in the short term: you have to think in time and big" LV

CONCLUSIONS

During our analysis we dealt with all the aspects concerning residential investments, with particular attention in this last case in which the holiday took place as a speculative phenomenon and therefore a rather risky investment, in the presence of a long-term rental that is always a strong workhorse and a medium-term rental that I personally see a very intelligent solution with little competition.

So we talked about the investor and all he needs to know in order to buy well and build a profitable "private business" that can provide revenue over time, until he gets passive, or managerial, items.

Throughout this process, the importance of programming, serious application and non-random conduct are being emphasized; from good basic ideas this is a time accumulated in the value of the property and meanwhile generating revenue.

We then definitely defined the do-it-yourself, intended as improvisation, attempted savings or disorder, as a very widespread, but very negative element as in the long run it does not work to build the foundations for stable and profitable work, giving only a few benefits in the immediate term, and on the contrary, often generating a series of problems which could have repercussions on the building itself or on a future sale.

On the contrary we have promoted the action of a few but good professionals of the various professions: it is no different differentiated from the really good ones, from the mediocre ones, but once done, we motivated what are the important values that these professional figures have, and above all done a portrait of how an investor can recognize and should themselves evaluate knowledge of their own.

Because ... let's not forget that the common goal of all this path is to optimize the investment, so you need to know how to recognize the right investment, be able to grab it, install a system that is profitable and, maybe one day, being able to sell: a lot of specializations required, therefore, for a very long laborious and complex job, which if it runs smoothly in any of these phases, turns into less profitable than expected, even down to being negative. In this sense, we find at the end, the real difference between do it yourself and a professional support system for an investor: provided that both situations can lead to success or failure, as the case may be, what is certain that a self-styled expert who "arranges himself" can only go so far; but a person with vision and organization, who knows how to make use of his knowledge, and where he wants to optimize his revenues, with the help of valid professional advice, always has an additional weapon, as well as a meter of comparison. Indeed, I would say that this is precisely the point: it will be able to express a clearly more targeted and broader firepower, and it will certainly achieve the objectives it had set itself and perhaps even go further.

START UP &

BUSINESS MANAGEMENT

Entrepreneurship and small business guide: how to manage your social media, marketing, ethics public policy and finally sell your brand.

Special focus on food & beverage

L.KELLER.

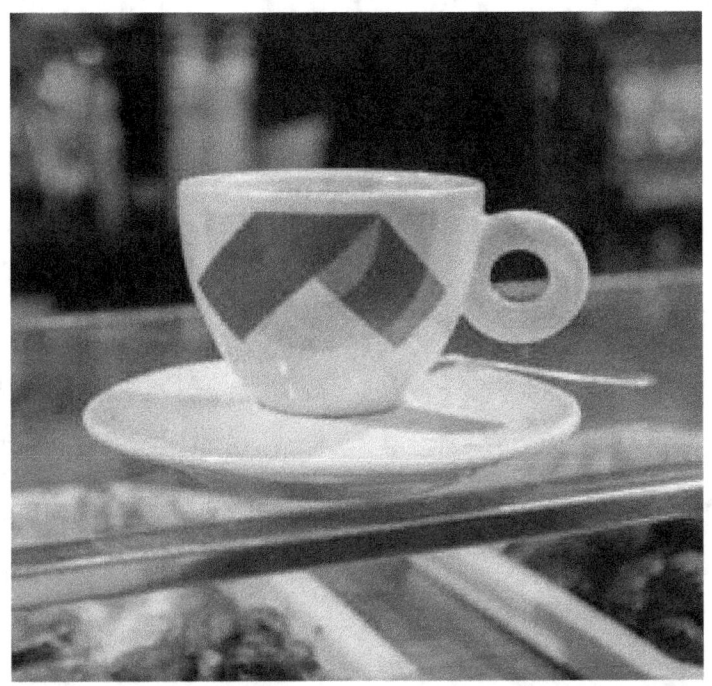

catering is one of the most powerful and widespread and explanatory examples of commercial activities carried out medium-small commercial properties

CHAPTER 1: BUSINESS FOOD & BEVERAGE AND ENTERTAINMENT

WHAT IS A COMMERCIAL ACTIVITY

We have talked during our theme of the commercial real estate part especially from the point of view of the investment on the property, but there is a part, not secondary attached to this branch, which deals more specifically with what can be done within these properties, ie commercial activities. Commercial activities are practically "the tenant who pays the rent of commercial properties", that is, the companies that manage the content within a property.

In this typology, among the best known activities we certainly find bars, restaurants, hotels and entertainment venues. They are among the "medium-small size" activities: for example, in larger areas we can find supermarkets / hypermarkets or, in smaller sizes, we can think of a professional studio or the typical retail store. Speaking of size, I am referring right now to the average extension in meters that an activity of those sectors can contemplate: instead the "size" at company level or the generation of monetary flows is different: in that case the extension is not always indicative because other types of factors intervene, which explain to us if an activity can be more or less profitable and therefore define its size in economic terms. The most common investor, and in any case a good part of the market for those who do business in commercial activities, often directs their attention towards the restaurant, or "food & beverage" and entertainment sector, which is the most commercial. and widespread: probably the most important of all exercises. In our analysis, approximating by default, we will focus more on this type of sector, even if the general rules that we will then outline often apply a little to all businesses without distinction.

WHO IS THE SUBJECT THAT ASSEMBLES A COMMERCIAL ACTIVITY

Normally there are two subjects when we deal with commercial properties: *first of all* the owner of the property, which depending on the importance of the investment can be a small owner of some store, rather than a magnate with considerable potential or professional companies that they deal with construction or commercial investments. The second subject that appears, which is a bit the protagonist of this part of the book, is the *tenant*, who can be, likewise, a small trader, rather than an affluent restaurateur with various points of sale (think of *franchises*), up to the big companies or tycoons that manage large hotel chains and supermarkets, for example. We have talked about two subjects, summarizing, owner of the property and **tenant**, because especially in small businesses the two locations are almost always distinct. Many times, however, they coincide, either because the manager of the business has "grown so much" that he was able to buy the property where he carries out the same (or in many cases various properties to replicate and scale his business model), or, looking at him from another point of view, because 'large companies have thought (in addition to building) to delegate: a part of their capital and human resources in this case will be dedicated exclusively to the direct management and administration of their companies, in the same properties they own. In these cases, obviously, we are not already talking about two subjects, but the subject is practically the same and economically and financially it has a logical sense of easy intuition: on the one hand, reducing costs, because if we look at it for the business side, it is it is completely different to go from paying a rent (disposable), to paying the installment of a mortgage, for example, to buy your own property. So seen from the side of the business, the step of buying a property to carry it out is almost always positive, when the position is openly favorable, because it "lightens the balance sheet" spread over several years with depreciation and a complete sense, ie squaring the circle, to corporate life. Seen instead from the point of view of the magnate who, for example, builds a large hotel (and then instead of entrusting it to a tenant in management, he decides to create his own directory to administer it personally), it is a choice that outlines the intention not to base your investment on a passive perspective (collecting the rent without doing any other action), but to take the path of a further *investment on the investment* and take the risk of setting up one's own business: if it is profitable, you will evidently benefit from the volume of business generated . In the latter case, it is clearly necessary to have a considerable economic strength to take on a double risk or such a demanding economic commitment; you also need very well-rooted skills within the business that you are going to organize, because the success of all the global investment depends on the outcome. In fact, should the activity not be profitable, not only would there be a loss of earnings (for passive rents), but there would be many other problems in the balance sheet: in that case the only way out would be to fall back on the management of a third party who carries out the same activity in a profitable way, and that allows the tycoon to return to have positive revenues, through the mere rent of the property. In the best case, there is also the hypothesis that << the big fish meets an even bigger one >> who wants to buy both the business and the property. If, on the other hand, neither of the two *exit-strategy* hypotheses described above occurs, our tycoon would begin to have significant economic problems.

WHAT COMES TO INSTALL A COMMERCIAL ACTIVITY

As an entrepreneur, I can safely tell you that setting up a business is one of the most risky things of all, among all the entrepreneurial categories, because it involves significant disbursements, implies advanced knowledge, requires the assistance of professionals and employees. Furthermore, it is necessary to guess, the place, the moment and the right system to dominate the competition, and many other things; and to make matters worse, an entrepreneur can do everything perfectly, but the possibility of "strange astral conjunctures" remains, so things don't work the same and crash, or they work but they don't give the desired results and therefore are insufficient to amortize the 'investment. Yes, because it is an investment: investing time, money and resources in a company: if all goes well, costs are amortized, wages and fees are paid and a dividend remains at the end of the year; the purpose of all this is practically to pay the expenses and have minimal earnings, increasing during the value of that brand or organization (to then resell it and have further earnings).

But what if things go wrong? If in 2020 for example we are forced to close our company 3 months for the *covid-19?* Will the once profitable business continue to be profitable or will it survive? The virus was a bad thing for the economy, but the economy thrives on ups and downs, real estate crises, financial crises, crises of any kind. They are called risks and an investor must keep in mind that they exist: nobody could imagine a world pandemic that would actually slow down or block the economy of hundreds of countries in the world. Pero 'has arrived, as well as past and future wars, and many other disasters, but economic activities have always continued to exist, because there are very entrepreneurial people who calculate everything, even that things can go wrong, and therefore they know that << today you win and tomorrow you lose >>, as in a long *football* championship, where maybe a team starts less favored, but then comes back and wins. And if he doesn't win there will be another adventure to undertake, another championship.

So the question is to do things measured, planned and well, and above all not to do them at random, like most people who, when they are tired of doing a certain job, suddenly one day they wake up and with all naivety, they convince themselves that they are the great *cheffs* for example, or the largest investors on the planet in any commercial field: they invest all their savings in randomly botched activities and often find themselves short of liquidity', because "an entrepreneur does not is invented "from today to tomorrow: they are just reckless attempts, and without any logic and destined for a crash, for an expert eye who recognizes them in advance only by how they are set.

WHAT YOU NEED TO KNOW TO SET UP A BUSINESS

I continue to insist that the first necessary requirement is to *know what it is about:* in the course of my professional activity I am seeing too many small or self-employed companies operating in *random circumstances* or with a really very deficient organization. This way of doing as well as being a losing well in terms of savings, proves to be a boomerang that will affect their lives, self-esteem and of course their savings, because the business has excellent chances of "falling apart". Absolutely, the first requirement is therefore to **be an expert in the business** that you are going to assemble, and certainly an enthusiast and lover of that world, up to know its more detailed facets. The second indispensable requirement is to **have the savings or liquidity to undertake;** very important thing to mark as a basic rule << if a company requires an investment of 100, get hold of 150 or 200 >>, because 'reserves could be needed in negative periods, in market fluctuations, in unexpected events, using them to keep it floating. Otherwise there is the possibility of arriving to lose everything. It is madness to buy an asset that has a cost equal to the available capital: it would mean that you are moving beyond your means.

Below we list all the other necessary requirements:

- **Check the current regulations:** cit. << with the help of a professional, contact the municipality of residence to request the permits necessary for the activity to be carried out. Through technical consultancy define criteria and rules and what can be done (and what can't), at the structural and plant engineering level. It is absolutely essential, in order not to risk making irreparable mistakes, to work authorized and in peace 'and to have clear ideas also in terms of costs and project>>.

- **Licenses:** acquire the main and accessory licenses necessary to carry out a regular activity. When working without a license or *border-line*, it could be profitable in the short run, but apart from committing an infringement, it absolutely will not be profitable in the long run let alone in the resale phase. There is a distinction to be made on licenses: if we return to catering for a moment as an example, there are obvious differences between having a bar, restaurant or disco license for example, or a hotel. For each area there are general and even municipal indications, on the basis the entrepreneur will have to comply with the requirements, so that the license is granted. And then, more on the technical side, there are category or safety limitations that determine the "goodness" of a deal. Not only that, according to the type, the days and times of opening change, but also the possibility of offering one service rather than another and also in detail the conformation of the commercial activity, which must be adapted to the rules according to the influx of people, location, and type of service to be performed. We will deepen this theme when we technically talk about how to prepare or renovate a commercial space.

- **Know how:** as the word says it is "the art of knowing how to do it": it is something that, either you know why you are experts in that profession (and have acquired the right skills), or that you must buy and it has costs. Together with the license and the *trade fund,* it is one of the main discriminants that determine the value of an activity. The easiest example to understand is the recipe for the best pizza or the best ice cream. Everyone makes pizzas and ice cream. But, have you ever wondered <<why the whole city

goes to pour in those usual two places, and nobody ever goes to the other 50? >> The answer is << because 'they have the best recipe for that product, and anyway the one that most like the market>>. So that "know-how" has a value and they can keep it secret (and continue to dominate the competition) or they can sell it by teaching *third parties* to do the same thing.

- **Commercial fund:** we mentioned it so we explain it in detail. In reality it is not necessary to start a new business; but it is essential to create it during the life of the company. We are speaking in a nutshell of the volume of business, or more simply of the "real customers who have a business": translated into numbers, of the volume of liquid revenue that these customers produce. The trade fund can be real (represented by the balance sheet and the volume of business expressed in a calendar year), or it can be potential, that is, the company's ability to expand and improve. Needless to say, the real trade fund is paid (and even salty at times) when the purchase of a business is perfected, while the potential is << like a great pair of shoes that are worn only for a wedding >>: you know it's there, you know it's worth it, but you'll never know if you can use it. In fact, the most important thing in the event of a transfer of ownership, with a significant outlay of capital, is to defend and confirm the numbers of the previous years: it is reasonable to think that new customers can be acquired, but old ones can be equally hypothesized that they can also be lost if you do not operate properly.

Once these priority aspects have been studied, what you need to set up a company depends on the activity you want to undertake: some will require **machinery** and **technical equipment,** others will also need **furnishings** and every aspect that has to do with the facade "on the public". Obviously, during the evaluation of an activity they are an important point and with a peculiarity: they almost never devalue (at least strictly speaking of machinery and technical equipment) and the reason is that they can be dismantled or moved and used in another store. , and therefore also be sold separately to similar companies.

Aspects to be kept in mind will then be the strategy of investing time and resources to increase the value of a **brand or commercial name:** if the business is newly established it will have to build an image and a reputation in its sector of competence: if instead it deals with a *sale of activities*, the brand becomes part of the negotiation, with the evident attribution of a certain value to be quantified. Let's not forget that, to start a business, if we are not owners of the property, we will have to find a rental agreement with the seller. It will be done on a multi-year basis to give the entrepreneur the opportunity to amortize the costs, and if he has a solid company, the benefit will be mutual, because the owner will thus guarantee an annuity, which can even be spent during the financing phase. of another building initiative, and obviously the investor will have time to repay his capital and generate a profit.

WHAT MAKES AN ACTIVITY WINNING

<< Position, position, position >>: you have to repeat it until you get tired, especially because for wrong price logics, many times you try to save money at the expense of the fundamental thing, undermining the investment from the ground up.

An important place then occupies the image, namely the brand and the attractiveness of the store from a strategic and aesthetic point of view (we will deal extensively in the second appendix with this theme).

Here we summarize the three fundamental pillars of an enterprise:

- **Product:** there is no profitable activity without a strong product that can outperform the competition, be it a physical product (such as making ice cream) or emotional (such as making fun). The product must always have the best value for money and follows the laws on supply and demand according to the location where it is undertaken. The banality of a product, the scarcity in quality terms or the price out of the logic of the market can alone sink any company, therefore in the planning phase they are very important strategies to be outlined in a long-term plan.
- **Service:** we can offer the best product in the world, and also have little competition, but if there is a lack of service, it could affect sales. To optimize and best express the potential of a company, you must have

strong organizational skills and put all the *cards* in their place. You need to know how to bargain the staff, in number and in quality, better to replicate the product in a scalar and systematic form. So not only must you be able to express a *one-time* production, but to repeat it, using people and means in order to generate lasting numbers over time, through effective and satisfactory quality standards, which are able to further enhance the product itself.

- **Planning:** it is possible to have the best product and the best service, but if you "sleep on your laurels", other people can overcome this model and become important and serious competitors to the point of even surpassing those who had wonderful ideas. The durability of the company over time is one of the most important things ever: short-term policies must be implemented, aimed at acquiring liquidity, but above all we must think "in the long run": when there are important outlays of money, in fact, there is a long-term amortization to always keep in mind and, before starting to make net gains, you must be able to last as long as possible, *primarily* to cover the investment costs. This can be gradual with gains over time, up to the achievement of the goal or can be resolved with a re-sale of the activity that covers all expenses and produces a profit.

In planning I also want to mention two very important subtitles such as **strategic choices and competition analysis.** Both are long-term policies and must be applied during the investment planning phase, *before taking the field*. The strategic choices are all those decisions which, based on experience and skills, must be made to study and classify the most important issues concerning planning: location for example. To be clearer, first when we talked about << position, position, position >> we were referring to first-rate, top-quality geo-localizations: to always be in front, in a geographical sense, but also of marketing positioning. Here instead, more specifically speaking of *location*, I want to refer to this specific example: << our store is geographically correctly positioned in the city center; it even has an important and successful brand and in social networks there is a lot of talk about us. Why don't we have the desired results? >>.

Provided that product, service, and all quality-price standards are correct, there may be reasons related to the point of sale or to the competition that have not been correctly evaluated:

- LOCATION: there is no unique guarantee of success, setting up a shop in the so-called "center". Always betrayed by the logic of price, aimed at saving money, many times I have seen choosing stores, not exactly in the center: I would say that << there is a center and a center!>>. Speaking to the inexperienced entrepreneur, he often tells you that his shop is perfectly located, but once you have made a simple inspection, it is quite easy and disheartening to see how his are "false illusions". To determine a centric area, it is not enough to take a map and draw a circle with a defined radius. The roads are not all the same, and even the same road does not guarantee the same productivity at the bottom *rather than at the head*. The assessments are always to be done in a physical and three-dimensional way, seeing the real situation. Even shops, which are side by side, we often notice that they have different profitability even if they do "the same job". The reason why one works (or not) can lead us back to the *goodness of the management* and the product-service, but many times the reason is purely linked to the property: a shop that makes a corner, rather than one with few windows, does not have not at all the same potential profitability. The same goes between a restaurant with a terrace, rather than exclusively indoors, or that has more or less seats: attention, then you have to convert this potential with other qualities. Often you have the skills but the location does not help due to the physical or organizational limits that it imposes on us. So a profound analysis during the design-purchase phase is by no means secondary, with experts who are able to anticipate, on the basis of their experience, certain situations which would then occur later, when it may already be late: when a shop is set up in a bad location it is difficult to remedy.

- COMPETITION: we never underestimate our competitors because one day they might not represent a factor, or another yes: let's not forget that they could sell the business to someone more proactive than they, or they could try to copy us, dispersing the customers and lowering our profits. In general, competition is something to always evaluate before undertaking, so as not to build *a cathedral in the desert* or on the contrary in the midst of other cathedrals all similar. One of the most innovative aspects that almost everyone underestimates, or does not contemplate, is the "exploitation of competition": it is a phenomenon that can be widely seen in large cities or large entertainment areas, and which deserves separate reflections. I am thinking of the typical example, in the *reconversion in large metropolises*, of what were once "the ancient markets": today they are leisure centers with restaurants, shows and much more; these are real huge buildings, but they can also be streets or areas, where a series of bars and restaurants or discos accumulate: all, with the various differences, offer a little the same product, namely *fun*. But let's take a more practical example: hypermarkets, which bring together a huge amount of retail stores, many of them similar in product and price line. This is a typical example of <<how to make a negative aspect like competition become a strength>>. The reason is very simple: a user is attracted by all the various possibilities offered by that situation and above all by comfort (is it another facet of the location: a place in a pedestrian area or a place with a private parking? A place easy to reach or an isolated place so as not to disturb the noises? All variables to be weighed in advance). So, most of the users go in search of those situations because << not even very clear what they are looking for >>, but they know they will find them: like when you go to a multi-screen cinema and decide the film at the moment to see: traditional cinema has disappeared.

So how do you work when you put yourself in such a market? Exactly as before, with the same rules and even more attention to quality and price to be competitive. We must certainly pay attention to the fact that the offer is not saturated for a certain type of product, with too many people undertaking in the same field or with similar products, and it is absolutely necessary to differentiate decisively by brand and service. Normally in this type of reality the models of *francising* are distinguished because they are highly competitive models, designed to proceed in certain ways and with certain pricing policies. So what is the fault of a leisure center? Although it is true that a model of this type helps and relieves an investor from the burden of attracting people within 1 KM of him, then it is also true that if he does not differentiate himself and does not have something highly competitive, he is destined to succumb even more fiercely. Then there is another negative point: if the center, the road or the area is not well managed, not well geo-located or not well advertised, working in a model of this type is even more complicated, because attracting people to 1 KM from your shop, then it becomes a necessity and very often, the possible bad image of the area is confused with the image of the store, and therefore the latter will have serious billing problems, as it will be difficult to convey the clientele in an unfamiliar or unwelcome place.

BUSINESS RISK

We have mentioned the possibility in which things do not go in the right direction: each type of activity assumes a different business risk, which depends on a virtual calculation on the volume of capital employed, on the economic period, and on the type of product or service. It is clear that the same business risk cannot be attributed to a family restaurant that operates in a property owned, rather than a hotel, which perhaps asks third parties for a concession to manage a certain number of years. There are therefore **companies of high risk or of lower risk:** those of high risk are all those that follow trends, for example (in terms of definition, *they come and go*) and when clearly we are then working out of context, unless that you don't have the strength to do it, you can have significant problems.

Other risky activities are those that have very strict regulations or a license that is not completely defined or that protects them from any disputes. The regulations unfortunately change over time and those who do not have everything expressly guaranteed and outlined could suffer problems related to bureaucracy or the changes that occur for economic or urban reasons. Even "news" or *start-ups* are high-risk activities: when you market a product that is innovative, it could work and become a fashion product (and therefore be very speculative), but it may also not work and therefore then and It is also difficult to correct the strategy in the race because the peculiarity that should have been a distinctive feature, then ends up also affecting a possible change. Without a doubt, however, there are as always in the life of the "workhorses" or *evergreens* that always work well or badly, that is, they have already been tried and tested over the years in different geographical areas and in different markets and are increasingly more or less profitable: residential real estate market, let's take an example to explain the concept, a long-term rental of an apartment compared to a "holiday rental": the first is undoubtedly a less bombastic and productive investment than the second, but with lower costs and with a practically minimal risk, in addition to being a safe haven asset, in comparison with the other type which is absolutely high risk.

COSTS, REVENUES, EARNINGS

This part is practically a small lesson on basic economics. We know that **costs** are all the expenses we use in carrying out a business: purchases, machinery, goods, personnel and everything else. Very often we forget to talk about the weather. **Time is one of the costs** most underrated in history. My innovative proposal is that << the time cost was included in the financial statements of companies >>: the result would be devastating, because many entrepreneurs would realize how little productive their organization is. The cost of time is practically "all the time lost and the capital invested" and blocked in an entrepreneurial activity: that is, the value that these would have if invested in another completely different initiative, or even in extreme cases in *doing nothing*. It is a modern version of the *opportunity cost*, and would allow us to understand "how many things had to be renounced" by spending time and resources in one company at the expense of another, but also of the family, or personal interests. Many times we focus so much on work that << for the anxiety of earning 100 we lose 150 >>; if we did the math well, perhaps it would turn out that there would have been enough, for a full life, a figure lower than that which we already had at the beginning, without facing any business risk. So when you are alone in front of the mirror, with *a pen and a writing pad*, let's remember to put everything under the heading costs, because leaving out certain aspects, not secondary, usually make up the accounts and are always positive even when they are not.

Revenues are the income that our business produces, but they are "false friends": especially in the retail trade, they give the impresario the impression of being well, of having solid revenues and resources; we must however remember that these are not because they are a partial datum; we cannot spend everything we collect. Revenues are used to cover costs and to reinvest, and then only ultimately to make a profit. So there are absolutely no liquids available, but they are resources to be handled with absolute intelligence. A bad management of the revenues can absolutely sink the *goodness of a* commercial *activity* and to go to intervene then there are always only two ways: either to reinvest to increase the turnover, and therefore to try that the cost-revenues relationship is more favorable; or cut costs (which is sometimes healthy to avoid unnecessary shopping); but when you get "to the bone", you cannot always touch them, not to undermine the correct functioning of the company. Finally, **the earnings** are therefore the positive result of a work path made profitably: if there are no earnings, the road is uphill, unless you are in a phase of physiological recession or you just have initiated or re-invested.

These three economic factors are always to be looked at from a medium-long term perspective and for this there are the financial statements, which are nothing more than the summaries by period of exercise, of the actions taken by a company. You should never ever confuse revenues with earnings: if, for example, a bar collects 1000 euros a day, remember the operator who does not have 1000 euros to spend in his pocket, but only earned the residual after taking out expenses such as: staff, electricity and water, materials, taxes, that day's depreciation of machinery, depreciation of its initial investment, rents, time, and a lot of other costs. Sometimes making this calculation we find ourselves with the understanding that *it's not worth the risk*.

Both corporate restructuring and reprogramming have well-defined rules and balances >> LV

CHAPTER 2: TOTAL RENOVATION OF A VS BAR-STAGING PROPERTY, WITH THE ABILITY TO REPROGRAM

DIFFERENCE BETWEEN RESTRUCTURING AND REMODELING

The investor of a business is normally a person with experience in the sector, and when this is not the case, normally he joins a company with someone who brings this essential value. Unfortunately, however, there are more and more people who re-invent themselves without any experience and, even worse, with resources below the minimum required level, they venture into companies that they then cannot carry out; most of the time due to lack of funds, or to changes in the market or lack of experience and planning. Always making the right example of catering, one of the most common and widespread mistakes is that, in addition to re-inventing oneself as restaurateurs, to believe oneself as great architects or interior designers, and even marketing experts, with results often not up to par and heavy consequences also from an economic point of view, the error or the principle is always the same: the savings policy. We have already mentioned that in commercial real estate "who spends more spends better", if we look at it from the perspective of the investment: because by buying something of value, we present ourselves to our personal race with the competition equipped with a *Ferrari*, and not with a small car to compete. If the logic of savings can be endorsed (but absolutely not married because there are very specific logics and rules also in that field) with a residential property, for its flexibility and for the fact of having a more standard, common and numerous user , on the other hand, with a commercial property (whether during the purchase of the property itself or during the planning of an activity), one must not remain "too short", in order not to make choices of secondary locations, accept obvious structural defects, or any factor that could potentially penalize our initiative; in this case the losses would be incalculable and the fate inexorably marked. Therefore, the selection of the property is important, among many in the different areas, taking into account all the factors that we discussed earlier in relation to the potentially profitable business. If in doubt about a position at the expense of another, it is always advisable to contact a professional in the sector to see the different possibilities or choices that the market offers, and to weigh the *goodness of one area* at the expense of another.

Once the content has been chosen, we then move on to a second phase which is decisive and then let's talk about what to put in the chosen shop: depending on the situations we will have to evaluate whether the store needs a radical change, which also affects installations and structure, or if it needs only a superficial reprogramming, intervening only superficially in the aspect visible to the public. In catering this type of intervention I like to call it **bar-staging,** which would be the commercial version of *home-staging* of houses, although with a considerable difference: what I mean as *bar-staging* is not limited only to the aesthetic aspect, perhaps accompanied by a programmatic evaluation of the type of investment and annuity to be assembled. In this case we are talking about something much more profound because the choice of colors or arrangement of a room or marketing or arrangement of furniture and resources can directly influence the increase in that company's revenues. We think of a beginner who decorates the bar, who has just bought, with very flat colors, tone on tone or even worse with colors that do not marry at all, and (without considering at the moment the range of the countless other choices he has to make on disposition, materials, machinery, lights, decorations...) he finds himself with a dull, monotonous and cheesy appearance bar, which certainly does not provide the right welcome and gives the impression of little professionalism. Let's think about how many times the same bar was subsequently sold to a brilliant and experienced entrepreneur who changed little and nothing (or on the contrary changed everything), and converted it into a *gold mine:* evidently this was a coincidence where the location was not so bad, but the subsequent choices made by the first investor were wrong. We can therefore say that those who have real experience, and real competence, can sometimes try to make up for it only and also dedicate themselves to an activity that is not completely his; in most cases one should rely on a professional in the sector to avoid making certain typical mistakes and above all to characterize and set up the store well.

For example, all supermarkets have real *teams* of people who dedicate themselves specifically to that: they do nothing but study, optimize and propose new spaces, new colors, new situations; they even often change the shelves because "behind" there is an economic reasoning and they have perhaps studied that certain products are sold more *if placed at the bottom rather than at the top*. If people who work at certain levels pay "good money" for what might seem like nonsense to most, because the novice investor who is starting now with commercial real estate or a business, decides heinously takes an additional risk and without experience, organize and decorate your own point of sale at random, or according to your personal logic? This would be very good if he bought a private house and wanted to live there: that he organizes it as he wishes, but then, if he were wrong, to pay duty during the sale, because people of common sense might not like it. But in the "commercial" it is not possible to reason according to a perspective of tastes, but of *sales*.

<< So we can define the necessary or vital restructuring or *bar-staging* in a commercial property, to characterize its activity and to optimize revenues >>.

But when to use one rather than the other technique? This varies greatly depending on the activity rather than the location and the need to prepare the store according to the law and according to the necessary safety standards. In general it can be said that: when there is a change of license or a change of activity, for reasons of law, but also for reasons of opportunity and updating of the property, an integral restructuring is carried out, perhaps negotiating with the owner of the property that still has to give consent. The concept of *bar-staging*, in spite of the name, applicable to all types of commercial activity, can be applied in all cases where you continue with the same type of license and no technical changes are required by legislation, and you simply want to give a shot of image and important substance to a store, to show first that things have changed, and later, to be able to express an economic revaluation of the store and the present activity, with consequent improvements from the point of view view of the entrances. We reiterate the importance of avoiding the *do-it-yourself,* which normally gives birth to anonymous stores, based on the logic of savings, which are not very functional at the time of working and replicating the product in a form that produces profitability.

If in the purchase of a house it was essential to evaluate the state of conservation of the property, in commercial properties it begins to be secondary because it is almost taken for granted that they will then be distorted or arranged and therefore we tend to market rustic properties, or finished but completely diaphanous and with standardized installations which can then be adapted to most commercial companies.

STEPS FOR AN INTEGRAL RESTRUCTURING

We have already seen how the first step is absolutely an analysis of the state of the property, not according to aesthetic criteria, but according to the expected updates necessary in a long period for installations according to the law.

Here are the most significant steps of an integral restructuring, the order of which is by no means secondary, because many times, those who are not experts in this sector, start for the half or for the end, and then find themselves redoing all in another way; needless to say, in doing so there is a huge increase in time and costs and often jeopardizing the previous work or the final result.

- **Check the current regulations:** << with the help of a professional, contact the municipality of residence to request the necessary permits for the intervention.

Through technical advice, define criteria and rules and what can be done (and what not), at the structural and plant engineering level. It is absolutely fundamental, in order not to risk making irreparable mistakes, to work authorized and in peace 'and to have clear ideas also in terms of costs and project. Recommended inspection for all technicians who will have to work: architect, master worker, electrician and plumber >>.

- **Study the new distribution of the spaces:** << compatibly with the project first of all define where the technical spaces of the bathroom and kitchen are located, and then concentrate on the main areas such as lounge or terraces or leisure space. You need to be very clear where to locate sensitive spaces before starting work, because all installations depend on it and, cascading, realizing belatedly an error can be impossible to solve or very expensive >>.

Particular attention, however, to the local policy: never underestimate the entry and the hypothetical distribution of the production points. The entrance is the business card of a store and must be large, attractive and easily accessible. Stores that have a bad entrance or architectural barriers are certainly having trouble billing large numbers. He must also be intelligent, and move the customer towards the most attractive and important we have. Sensitive production spaces are the most important spaces after technical spaces: the first inevitably affect the distribution of the store, but these are the ones that will discriminate whether we sell or not. In the very intuitive example of a bar, it is vitally important where the counter (and kitchen) is placed for example: not only that, the collections can change according to the size of the counter, the shape, the color, the comfort and the type of session (or not) that you set; follows a lot the logics about the types of bars that are going to be built, therefore an expert will not only look at aesthetic criteria, but also of consistency and functionality at work in order to increase the takings.

- **Demolition:** << is the first active phase of the work. We will have already studied whether there are old walls to be demolished or old installations to be abandoned. At this stage it is appropriate to protect or remove the furniture and parts that you intend to save, so as not to damage them because it normally produces really annoying dusts at the time of cleaning and inconveniences due to the work of several people in the same environment. It is appropriate to clear the area as much as possible to facilitate the work and then be able to easily intervene in the removal of doors and fixtures or demolition of walls, decommissioning of furniture that is of no interest and anything else. If the wooden floor, for example, is one of the things that can be saved, protect it to avoid direct scarring for moving furniture or even unwanted, for the simple passage with the possibility of small debris under the shoes >>. Of course it is true that unlike what happens in residential property, as we have highlighted, there is a tendency to have diaphanous spaces in order to avoid demolitions but go directly to a redistribution of spaces with internal divisions.

- **Construction of new walls:** << if provided, there will be the redistribution of the surface with new walls that will delimit the new size of the rooms. According to the uses, they can be made with blocks, with wood or with the most economic and widespread solution and with the best aesthetic result: the plasterboard, properly insulated >>.

Also in this case, the choice of distribution and separations in a commercial property is far from trivial: it must respect certain logics of breadth and design, above all to give users a feeling of being able to breathe. Therefore preference for diaphanous spaces, even if we record that in certain activities, the separation of some more intimate environments can be a stylistic choice, but also an economic one, sometimes important: we think of a reserved and intimate room in a restaurant or certain delicious corners, for to offer customers certain differences in atmosphere, or if we think of the economic side we think of discos and *prive'*: we offer exclusive services, with an increase in management costs for the company, in exchange for notoriously higher prices for the service offered in that space: these are details that aim to differentiate customers and to have a different economic entrance.

- **Electrician and plumber:** << contact the electrician and plumber who, assisted by a worker, will have to "cut" the walls and the floor and then channel their pipes. Both technicians will have to prepare the installations according to the law and according to the project, using the appropriate materials, and trace their installations from the command point to the central plant. The electrician will have to discuss about how you want to equip and equip the house to understand the necessary power and adapt an authorized electrical panel, then making the related requests to the administration company. Both will propose ideal points of water and light in the most common points, according to their criterion, but here also the user will have to give his opinion according to his needs and the result will be a mix of requests, standards and advice on the basis of experience of other previous works. Also contact specialized technicians, for example that of air conditioners to have the desired machinery ready >>.

The main difference between residential and commercial property is that commercial property systems are often "exposed", both for a significant reduction in the cost of the work, and because they are lost to sight in the large space or can be camouflaged in full industrial-style aesthetic, quite cleared through customs today.

- **Carpenter, installer, tiler, gas engineer, carpenter:**<< call these skilled workers for the realization of works that cannot be damaged, even if you continue to work in the house. Barriers, stairs, ornaments, counter-ceilings, bathroom and kitchen tiles, floors can be made only if it is not a delicate surface that can be damaged, such as for example wood and similar surfaces: in this case it is expected that almost everyone has finished and poses, or alternatively poses and covers themselves to protect it, but at the risk of ruining it. Similarly, the first finishes and details can be made. There is always to keep in mind that if you choose a so-called *floating* floor, that is superimposed on the existing floor, this installation must be done before commissioning the doors because the height of the floor will obviously vary and consequently also the size of the new doors to be requested on assignment. Normally we tend to leave the change of doors and windows last (being able for safety reasons), so as not to run the risk of ruining new materials due to the great coming and going of people and above all the transport and assembly of new furniture or antique furniture that had been moved. The fixtures and doors and walls are then finished with the relative *skirting boards* or decorations, which have the function of protecting the materials and hiding any cutting or installation defects >>.

- **Painter:** << normally he is the last to arrive and is in charge of fixing all the small defects and then covering them first with white, and then giving personality to the house with color. In theory, he should paint in white before the assembly of the new furniture and once mounted, dedicate himself to color: this would facilitate the times and the task of the painter, but if it were not possible, you can do everything later >>.

Unlike what happens for residential properties, here the painter must be *much more an artist than a performer.* always maintaining certain quality standards, he must collaborate with the investor and the designer to find suitable chromatic solutions that reflect the distinctive features of the company, and therefore have to do with a defined marketing strategy, and then highlight the important points depending on the activity to be carried out. Therefore it must make more *quantities* and be effective; maybe he can afford to be slightly less shrewd (as opposed to what happens in the residential field), because what will be decisive *is the general appearance of the intervention.*

- **Furniture, lights, decorations:** last but not least, we find the fun, but not secondary, part of beautifying the place: many people often do it "by chance" by mixing styles, colors and materials that are inconsistent and ruining something that it was thought and that it had an important cost.

If it is important in homes, a detailed study is essential in the premises:

- LIGHTS: they must take into account also and above all consumption (as well as all the machinery with which we supply the premises) because there are companies that count many opening hours; luckily the technology comes together offering a great variety of neon or led lights, with great energy savings and aesthetic solutions and colors of all kinds. In general, then there is to reflect on warm or cold lights depending on the type of work that will be carried out. Needless to say, cold lights are generally brighter and also highlight the flaws in the room; warm lights are generally used more for night activities because they also affect the atmosphere of the store.

- FURNITURE: the furnishing of a shop consists of everything that is visible to the public, and therefore contemplates any seating, leisure space, entrance, public service spaces such as exhibitors or counters and customer attention. All these visible spaces must be arranged in a functional way, in order to allow the correct performance of the activity and respect a certain aesthetic taste.

There is no doubt that there are situations in which machinery, in certain *industry* styles, is sometimes integrated into the concept of commercial real estate as part of the furniture: we think of the large vacuums located in large supermarkets or shops, so powerful and invasive to the eye that over time have made fashion, marking a style of commercial property with exposed systems. We think of a brewery or a large professional wine cellar, where sometimes there are even real cisterns at sight and guided tours are organized to explain the various stages of processing. Even in a restaurant, for example, there is a pizzeria area or an "open" kitchen area, and therefore in these cases there is the transformation of the technical space into an absolute first floor space inside a room. It is obvious that for these reasons it must be located and designed so as to be easy and at the same time to have an aesthetic function.

_ DECORATIONS: decorations are all those accessory elements that give personality and uniqueness to a shop. They may be some particular furniture or lights with the function of drawing attention, but also paintings, statues, vases, areas, original details aimed at creating a kind of context or choreography. They must be harmonious with the rest and characterize the store so that it is attractive and original for customers. The keywords in this area are balance and consistency: decorating with something that loads the environment too much is harmful. Everything must have a harmonious shape and be noticed with the right importance. If something is not noticed, neither individually nor does it serve to contextualize a specific choreography, this often means that it is too much.

- **Exterior of the room:** << it is the only item that can be independent from the rest and can have a non-consequential value: that is, it can be reformed or not even later or in a different time space. According to the technical characteristics of the house, it is necessary to intervene on roofs, façades, gardens, entrances, accessory spaces and gates. Clearly this type of intervention requires "a whole separate discussion" which is not part of the themes of this book, but has much more to do with architecture >>.

The exterior of a commercial premises must also have the function of drawing attention. It must include **a sign** with the distinctive features of the company, whose characteristics must be aesthetic and also highly visible. The name and logos of the business will be on the sign and the type of product or service it offers must be clear.

We have already talked about the importance of the **entrance,** which characterizes the transition between exterior and interior.

We have already mentioned the fact that it is advisable to have accessory spaces outside the store, which will be exploited according to the activity; but one of the almost essential things of a commercial property is the ease of **parking.** In fact, if it is true that there are properties of this type also in pedestrian areas (where however there are always paid parking lots in the immediate vicinity), having a private parking, attached to the store, is always one of the strong points that can determine its success: the simplest case to think about is "weekly shopping": which supermarket would be successful without parking? How would customers be able to carry their purchases if there was no possibility to park in the immediacy? Another important case is that of a fast food restaurant: if it aspires to make large numbers, it cannot be located in the absence of a car park or pedestrian zone (with a high traffic) because its model especially leverages on the *convenience of people.*

BAR-STAGING

From a general overview, we defined *bar- staging* as a "less invasive intervention" than the total renovation, but equally effective: this in fact will not concern so much the room itself (intended as property), but rather the activity that takes place at the interior with a repositioning or change of furniture, colors, lights and perhaps the redistribution of the main points of attention to the public. Clearly, this intervention must observe stylistic and balance rules that only a professional or a very experienced person can give him: it is very frequent to see how the *do it yourself* infects inexperienced investors, who many times do not follow any logical canon and reproduce environments absolutely lacking in personality and consistency. It is a bit like when you take photos at a wedding: no matter how advanced the technology has been in recent years, you still pay a professional for large amounts, because you immortalize those moments: it is normal, that being an unrepeatable moment, you don't want to make a mistake, and you know perfectly well that these can produce hundreds of shots of remarkable quality, to the detriment of those who, with the do it yourself, could take a dozen really good photos. In fact, the professional has such training that he knows how to ignite the subject well, add certain details that detach, use some techniques (for example the lights) to accentuate certain atmospheres and organize the spaces in the way that the subjects stand out. The reprogramming intervention in *bar-staging* is the same, because if done in a professional way it can absolutely make a store shine, in a way so superior that the practice of *do-it-yourself* is absolutely noticeable "at the sight" of any profane, when making a comparison.

There is, however, one more *step* that differentiates a professional job in this field and it is the application of a change that reflects on corporate profitability: having already talked about the relevance of the counter in a bar, we take that example to highlight how much this distinctive element could influence profitability and also the geography and layout of the store. << We know that the bar counter is a cornerstone and we have thought of a hypothetical location; are we sure it is the correct one? >> The counter is perhaps the most distinctive character of this type of exercise and should always be located in a close-up view, completed by the back counter where you usually place bottles or glasses, or use it as a decoration. If we think of a rectangular-shaped shop, it is not the same thing to place it at the bottom, rather than at the beginning, rather than frontally or sideways: they are absolutely decisive and difficult decisions for an inexperienced person, because he would lose too far of importance and would be difficult to reach in certain types of night bars, irreparably lowering the volume of sales. Too close to the entrance could be a dramatic aesthetic solution and not entice you to enter the main hall, which would always appear a dark and distant place. << And if we put it in the middle of an island? And if we talk it straight from the side? >> Any decision will change the economic result of this company for better or for worse because the main product of this type works in this area. The *do it yourself* in these cases could be lethal, because we tend to think only of the aesthetic sense and not of the practicality of the work or the profitability of the shop. There are also other criteria to be taken into account, to avoid seeing unpleasant situations, such as "a counter near the bathrooms" (where even smells or embarrassing situations are suffered at sight), or too far from the kitchen, which implies more personal and less control. Then we want to talk about the choice of whether to put or not to put stools that determines the type of clientele you will have? When the customer "eats and drinks on the counter" it is clear that there is work to be done in a different system than the classic table service. Let's talk about the color or the materials? Apart from an aesthetic criterion, we should evaluate the cost and durability of one of the main actors of this activity.

We could continue for hours talking about every single detail of a counter, and you think we are only at the beginning because then we have tables and chairs to discuss other hours, mezzanine or separate room, open kitchen or not, classic service, self-service or table service with show. Entry of a certain type rather than another. Terrace. Lights. Decorations, etc ... for each element we could spend hours discussing: however the main concept is only << **each choice in a commercial premises is directly reflected on the turnover** >>, because it can make the tasks more or less easy to carry out, or it can make a place more or less pleasant and attractive. This does not mean that a perfectly set bar necessarily functions, because subsequently personal and managerial factors of the various entrepreneurs come into play, but surely, setting it up incorrectly is like starting with a *handicap in an obstacle course.*

<< The practicality added to an excellent aesthetic result and the optimization of the revenues through the organization of the spaces >>: this is what is what I have called *bar-staging*.

The novice investor almost always thinks only of aesthetics, and in most cases (not being a professional in this matter, dazzled perhaps by good ideas), he does not have the competence to develop and execute them correctly. The result is often called *monotony*, with fairly standard and uninteresting rooms; even worse when they are not very functional. Think of those who have had in the past (today there are stricter regulations and certain things are not practicable), << the brilliant idea of placing a restaurant kitchen in the underground warehouse >> or upstairs, simply with the aim of increasing the number of tables by a few units. Space is undoubtedly very important, and the more tables you have, the more potential collections you can express. But can you imagine the inconvenience of such a solution and all the consequences it entails? Mind you, there are certain situations where it is necessary, especially in the city in old or small places where solutions must be invented, but being able to choose this is one of the typical solutions that "will make you lose money" because they will probably require more staff or the installation of a freight elevator, never solving the problem of practicality and slowing down the service offered.

There is nothing randomly located in a commercial space, not even the details that seem more insignificant.

Furniture and decoration are also not secondary: have you ever entered a place that aesthetically has an appearance and then once inside, feel completely out of context? Contradictions. The inexperienced entrepreneur often moves in this way: abuse of the *do it yourself* and then when he sees that the results do not arrive, he begins to listen to all the voices: << why don't you add this? >>, << why don't you change the other? >>: its trajectory therefore passes from "having mounted a monotonous room" to converting it into a "nonsense room" because it adds and changes details or objects (very often also good and expensive), which however is not they marry with each other, until you get to a non-homogeneous mix or jumble style disused objects, put at random (for the record there are rooms in this style, but they are absolutely studied: every object or thing "put at random", in reality is not 'not at all, because' everything follows rules and a coherence of style and design).

What is meant by this argument? That setting up a commercial space so that it is ready to host an activity is not at all a question that can be "done well", because every mistake affects work and entrances. Activities already involve many risks and many variables by nature: why add a problem? Just to save something or for an *eagerness* to lead? There are experts in what we have called *bar-staging*: if we speak only of aesthetic criteria, for example, a *home-staging* professional or a good decorator or general architect can design the room without any problem. With respect to the unskilled investor without experience, surely at least it would be nice: and in fact **it is the error that many commit**, because they stop halfway: there are beautiful bars certainly designed by a professional who, however, normally dedicates himself to the market residential: for multiple reasons the result can be absolutely pleasant, but with enormous problems from the point of view of corporate life: beauty is not the only determining factor. So to get a superior result you would have to contract a professional *bar-staging*, or **remodeling of a commercial premises** (therefore you are a decorator or an architect but who are purely trained in the commercial field), but here we are already in the field of "rare goods" because few have the skills to do such a job. You should certainly have drawing experience, to organize the spaces, but also experience of the type of business to be carried out and commercial marketing experience and many other types of experience. I personally, for example, have all the skills and experience necessary to perform a job of this type, given my professional trajectory, but only in the field of catering or leisure premises; for example, if I had to do it in a supermarket I would not feel comfortable, because apart from the aesthetic criteria, I do not know that type of activity and therefore I would not know how to optimize it: for this reason my "specialty" and my advice I only offer in the theme in which I have specific skills: that is, leisure and *food and beverage venues.*

Large companies, for example, have their own team that only deals with setting up one store after another. We also think, for example, of *franchises* which can be very large (or small) stores, in any case, replicated in many different places while maintaining the same distinctive features, the same aesthetic and structuring rules depending on the original design of the *parent company,* adapted to the technical limits of the property being furnished. They even have parameters, so tight that many times they discriminate certain areas by location, property characteristics and limitations (the parent company refuses to proceed with the operation often occurs). Normally smaller companies solve the problem of a professional decoration of a room, **with a mixture of**

figures and a union of intent: the owner dictates the guidelines and explains what type of business he intends to set up; then there is an architect or decorator who takes care of the aesthetic part; if you are not forward-looking, the part of ductility and functionality linked to the organization of work remains a bit uncovered, something that is compensated with time and experience, or that should be entrusted to a professional third party, who is dedicated exclusively to that.

SCALAR INVESTMENTS

The truth is that there are many inexperienced investors: but in other cases, we find entrepreneurs who are very prepared and have had such good results that they are able to scale their business quickly. We have already talked about *franchising* as the most intuitive system to reproduce what has been successful in a store, reproposed in a sane way in other locations. This is the most linear model of **scaling** a commercial **investment.** We think of hotel chains rather than supermarkets: once the first is assembled and produces high yields, the easiest thing to do is to replicate the same model at a distance of non-competition, thus minimizing risks, because it is adopted a winning project, and trying to control the territory: these are the first two steps to build a network of sales outlets and therefore dominate the market with your own brand. Among other things, there is also a tax issue to be analyzed: we all know that the first two years of an activity are customary that they result in losses due to the *start up*, due to market resistance and due to the amortization of the investment that weighs on the budget: in a nutshell you pay duty to be in the beginning. But then if all goes well, breakeven points are reached and then the first profits appear. Without the spirit of offending anyone, no entrepreneur likes to pay too many taxes and when a company begins to produce a lot of profits, an investor must ask himself whether it is better to pay taxes (which would be a dry expense) or to reinvest. It could reinvest in the same starting activity and renew itself, but that I took for granted in the analysis, as normal practice to keep a store updated. The other *chance* he has is to invest in another property or another business: he would therefore reduce the taxation because in this case it would be a matter of putting the new operation at "cost", and his profits would be zeroed in the financial statements. This practice is totally legal and is not at all a way to get around taxes; think of a supermarket that reinvests to open another: it will surely put the operation at cost and therefore will not pay taxes on the previous initiative. Why do the institutions allow him such an operation? Think for example of how many jobs this operation generates and how much additional economic activity. In turn, these factors lead to new taxes or a new reversal, if there are new budget profits, and so on. It is clear that the system is correctly assembled to promote entrepreneurial activity, work and economic life, with all the benefits that result from a positive activity.

There is however another system of doing business and "it is not replicating the winning model", but on the contrary **differentiating**, to have control over the whole of a sector, rather than to diversify the risks, rather than for the convenience of market: it is not unusual for some famous brands of specific products to start producing something different or that has nothing to do with the original product; I am reminded of the example in the *Yamaha* brand for example, a very famous manufacturer of motorcycles of all types. Perhaps not everyone knows that to scale their investment, for example, the same brand also produces other things, such as engines for boats, which have little to do with street bikes. The *reason* that moves this is the same that we have just explained about taxes and re-investment, but in this case the way is to differentiate the product. As for commercial properties, the contextualization could be exemplified in this paradox: << I am the owner of a very famous coffee shop and I have great profits: what do I do? >>: one of the possible ways would be to open another identical coffee shop in another location; but why not think of a business lunch restaurant instead? And so we move on to "control" the market in a wider range of time and with a clientele with superior economic capabilities. If there were further profits from the two initiatives undertaken, and you wanted to optimize your revenues, by leveraging marketing, you could expand the restaurant's activity and convert it also for evening work, where a higher price policy is applied. But it's not over: on another property, always using the profits of the assets, you can decide, in the end to even invest in a disco. With such diverse and independent activities, but belonging absolutely to the same niche (*food and beverage and leisure*) and good marketing, you can absolutely "control" a good portion of the public, loyal and of large numbers, because the market in that sector is being dominated with contiguous operations with each other: paradoxically a customer could spend a day of 24 hours in the companies described, sometimes even without even knowing who the property is. 'Subsequently, from this customer base, through the knowledge, a virtuous circle of customer turnover and all that will follow will be generated. In a nutshell, in the "commercial" there is no limit to the scalability of the business: the only detail is that you have to be truly prepared in your job, meet a truly productive system and then organize to reproduce it better than the competition.

marketing must convert and sell in the long run

CHAPTER 3: MARKETING FOR COMPANIES

DIFFERENCE BETWEEN MARKETING AND ADVERTISING

These two concepts are often confused with each other as if they were a synonym, but in reality they are to be considered "each other's container". Marketing not only includes advertising, but it is all << **a set of actions and plans through the qualification of a result** >>, which in most cases connected << the increase in the value of a brand or brand >> (with economic consequences for the reference company).

The inexperienced entrepreneur translates it, trivializing it, often with << buy an infinite number of advertising products>>, or double ads and spots, because he mistakenly thinks that this means *"do more marketing"*: this definition is wrong, because << marketing is only one>> and has no quantity (advertising is measured in quantity, marketing is not). It is a unique project which, through studied and varied actions, linked together, generate a result.

Let's take some very intuitive practical examples: << rate 20 *radio and television* announcements and updates increased to 100 is marketing medium? >> Sincerely, if these are the last words of the discussion, the answer is negative: this simply made of advertising costs on average, which in the short term can also assume a result, because it is statistically true that more announcements are made and you have more chances to be seen (what I am using is a very simplified model because we should also discuss the quality of these ads and where they are off It is therefore called **"advertising" << the act of increasing visibility >>** through actions, without there necessarily being an overall strategy other than the "purpose of directly increasing sales": it is possible, if incisive, to intervene in increase liquidity in the short term, but in the long run its benefits are difficult to measure. Advertising makes sense when you promote something in concrete, for example an event or a novelty, and you want to get this information as quickly as possible to a large number of possible users. Let's take the case of an entertainment room: the advertising result is measurable when, through our announcements, many people will gather at a concert; in this case its effectiveness is proven. However, once the concert is over, its function will be practically exhausted and therefore it may have no effect on the future:

it should therefore be counted as a cost, necessary to organize that event. When proceeding with the analysis of the costs of this action, it will be necessary to see if it was worth it or not. On the contrary, on the other hand, the strategy of "making *live music* concerts" can be considered a marketing strategy for this type of exercise: it is probably insufficient for the needs of an entertainment company to function, but if it is combined with other long period (which we will see later), can be absolutely successful. So where does it differ from advertising? Simple: advertising is the means by which to organize an event, but the fact of building a history of events and of continuously recycling people in that place is a marketing action: the aim of making music thus becomes an opportunity to attract an audience that then stations, spends and has fun and then in turn attracts other people for the next event. All marketing choices involve costs, but which are aimed at forming a general plan that must **lead to increase the company's turnover and brand value.** Now it is easy to understand how marketing is actually the "instigator" of an action, and advertising is only a "performer", that is, a mere tool (among other things, not the only one), to achieve it, but everything according to well studied logics in advance.

MARKETING POST COVID-19

Knowing how strategies will evolve following such large changes is very difficult; what can be hypothesized is that the systems will change but not the substance and the logics that have always guided the winning business choices from the period of the "industrial revolution" onwards.

Let's try to imagine how markets change and consequently marketing in a post-virus period. Clearly our attention will be mainly focused on real estate investments and commercial activities.

<< I will not go on to tell you about the Corona-virus as such, because unfortunately we have all experienced the period of this world pandemic that has just affected us and that has changed our lives, forcing us to take refuge in the house to escape them, but hopelessly blocking the direct economic system of different countries (indirectly affecting the entire world economy as a result). We all already know where it was born and how it spread, we know the numbers of the victims and the limiting measures that we had to take, but we don't

know exactly the numbers of the economic damage yet: we may perhaps have a personal idea, which varies from company to company a company, according to what was invoiced in 2019 and will not be invoiced in 2020, but the consequences of all this will not be limited to 2020 alone and exactly it is difficult today to estimate how much it will affect the following years.

Do you wonder this consideration? Perhaps someone had deluded themselves that with a few months of isolation all this would pass and it could be cataloged as a bad memory to be forgotten as soon as possible. Unfortunately it will not be so and even if they are only theories, I will try to explain them to you in the most practical way possible, through examples, so that everyone can ask their own questions. "Questions": yes, because no one is currently able to give absolute answers; one can only make assumptions.

What is certain is that nothing will be the same as before, because the contemporary world has found itself vulnerable to something that not even Bin Laden and his terrorist organization had come to do: in 2011, in fact, the terrorist acts had made the most supportive and united world, strengthened the desire to unite and collaborate to overcome what had been a vile attack. It was almost as if terrorism had been defeated, apart from that by the US military, by itself, as it brought about the union under the flag of the United Nations, with an unimaginable sense and desire for freedom and pro-positivity: the terrorists' followers had frightened, but they had certainly not blocked the world: the world instead blocked it covid-19 nine years later. In fact, this bizarre virus, underestimated by all, has gone quite hidden for months, disguising itself with strange episodes classified then as simple "pneumonia" in the worst cases or spreading among the asymptomatic. He was not known, and therefore nobody feared him, and at the beginning he positioned himself strategically, to then appear officially in China and subsequently in Germany with the patient or European; but not officially he was already around the world, probably from the second half of 2019, sly, silent. Then when the "bubble" exploded and the numbers collapsed, this bizarre enemy was given name and surname, and then the fear began, above all because we discovered that we could not face it, neither from a medical point of view (no vaccine), nor were we ready with the facilities and numbers to deal with it from the point of view of the health emergency, with the various national systems *overloaded* in a few weeks. This time the enemy had hit his target: not only the direct victims, but all the consequences: *fear outside the front door.* To demonstrate the weakness of an entire nation, even of many countries. And above all, to separate, given that it was one of the few wars in which the peoples, after reaching stability, felt more divided than ever: the various nations did not react in a uniform form, but in drops, they implemented very different in timing and reactions. There was solidarity and it is true, but late and in most cases not very effective.

People have reduced themselves to locking themselves up frightened (and not understanding) in their homes, without even having often embraced a family member. It was one of the few wars that divided "before, during and after", also because << loving each other in that moment hurt ", that is, you had to separate and distance yourself to stay safe: any contact could have been risky. Months of this psychological and media massacre that will change the way we perceive life forever. Unfortunately, those who will surely constitute the most significant legacy will not be good intentions, easy to forget in a few months, but the economic and social consequences of the thing >>.

- **HOW THE REAL ESTATE MARKET CHANGES FROM 2020 ONLY** << At the end of 2019 I was going to record my recurring videos of updates on the situation of the real estate market in my area of competence, and well in advance I highlighted how much the forecasts of the following year would have been clearly alarming, predicting and anticipating a real estate crisis at the end of 2020: probably, I was wrong, but only because I was optimistic, I could not know of the virus that inexorably did nothing but anticipate the steps that would have occurred anyway for other reasons: the already mentioned Brexit, tour operator crisis, new Middle East spotlight and holiday home inflation. I therefore expected the approach of an economic crisis (and of a real estate reflex) that would lead to the devaluation of the properties within a year, and *first of all* those less positioned or distinct. As well, we are all clear by now, this process is already underway and everything is taking place very quickly. The peculiarity of this crisis is that it will have gone from a final of the year 2019, with very high prices to a beginning of 2020 with prices in sharp fall: all in the space of a few months and without notice. This in the residential field, where however there will be differences for very unique properties or for particularly interesting areas; it will probably be a catastrophe for commercial activities, of which a good part had to make drastic decisions, such as "closing its doors" or selling, perhaps at a very devalued price, in a hurry.

In the future, there will probably be a kind of **natural selection,** where those who do not have a certain professionalism or economic strength are destined to disappear from the market. In a sense, not all evils come to harm because this will lead, in the long run, to higher average quality and less "inflation", but during this change there is always someone worthy who unfortunately cannot "stay on your feet "(and someone who is less deserving than with artifices or economic solidity resists and therefore follows the best).

The important issue will therefore soon be that of liquidity. How is this reflected on investments? The most obvious consequence is the lowering of prices on sales, but there is also to be taken into account that prices also go down because there are fewer people with the opportunity to buy. In reality, the market will return to being a market of "buyers" (that is, where the buyer is holding the negotiations), because there are already many investors who were organizing and were not moving, waiting for the favorable market swing to buy. as soon as the prices were more accessible. In fact, in recent years there had been a fairly widespread arrogance on the part of the owners in fixing the values of their properties, and the good investor had stopped buying, "letting buy" only private individuals, who had personal interests, rather than contingent needs, and they certainly could not wait years for a business cycle to change. So to think that there are no buyers is wrong, but now **the type of buyer will change:** be careful, however, not to be fooled by the "myth of the investor". Many times we have heard opinions of sellers who defined their properties or businesses as << perfect for an investor >>, often supported only by their personal desire or interest to believe in this thing. Investor does not mean "dumb". Quite the opposite! The veteran investor, for example, is the exact antipode of the owner, that is to say, through his communication, that << everything is worth less, really, than the value that is being attributed to him >>. So on the one hand the owner has a tendency to swell; on the other, the aggressive investor has a tendency to demonstrate that it is worth much less in the market. How can owners ever hope in vain for investors as saviors of the homeland? The reality is that they are investment professionals and are not used to buying off the market.

<< Sometimes I have been offered marketing assignments, for ancient buildings, at a price that we define in this example as 100. The goal that according to the owner I should have found was "an investor", *because a private individual could not afford that outlay >>:* the first thing you do in these cases, look on the agenda for the first 5 numbers of the most important investors in the city and start calling. Unfortunately, often the answer is << Thanks, but I'm not interested, because I'm selling "the new one at 110", and therefore it costs too much. In fact, I would buy what you offer me, in a price between 50-60 because maybe it is worth 70. So considering all the expenses, at this price you propose is uneconomical >>. It is quite obvious that *I refuse regardless of assignments of this type*, just after having

informed the owner of responses of this type (and having seen that his reaction is absurd: << then let's try to lower it to 95 >>. << But if it is 70?! >>). I hope it is quite clear that for this type of owner, **the investor will never be a resource**, just as this property will never be purchased by an investor (and probably under these conditions not even by a private individual), because it is out of the market.

So I'm painting a very problematic scenario, where there will be an absolute need for a change of *mind-set* by the owners and responsibility by the buyers: the former will necessarily have to adapt to the market, unless they decide and can afford to wait a new economic cycle in a few years, and the latter will not have to "pull the rope too much" and present absurd offers. From the balance of the two positions, the real estate system will return to turn and produce, and surprisingly it could be one of the first to recover, at least in the residential area in certain geographical areas. Everything therefore depends on the *mind-set* and the balance between supply and demand: the faster the adaptation to the new market, the faster the transactions will return >>.

- **SOCIAL AND ECONOMIC CHANGES** << I see that the paralysis of the real estate system is therefore not expected, more simply a change, on the other hand a radical change in the uses and customs of people and the consequent economic shift of wealth by sectors is very certain.

Social and economic changes sectors. As we learned in the letter written by covid-19, this experience will change certain systems and ways of thinking, and above all it will concern entrepreneurship and the way of thinking about corporate life. Perhaps the real function of the virus, in the end, will be to really bring us into the XXI century, because until now everything had remained exactly the same as the XX century, with a slow and inexorable expiration of products and service in general. Is this the occasion for a real economic-industrial revolution?

The first effects of this experience have been seen in commerce and services. As the first activities were blocked by the restrictive decrees, they closed the physical store and organized or strengthened an existing *online trade*. Obviously, bars, for example, cannot prepare us a *cocktail online*, nor offer us aggregation and fun; but apart from these cases, let's think about the marketing of clothes, housewares, products in general, and food products themselves (many people have started to request more supermarket home service for fear of going out to buy firsthand): previously only a small niche used these *online services* in this sense, but with limited confinement, for months, they have become more and more accustomed to searching the internet for a product and to request it for shipping. In this sense, it is plausible to think that companies of this type, for the future, will further strengthen this branch, and this could also change the logic of the stores, which have always worked until yesterday. It is quite obvious and obvious that there will therefore be a lot of changes from an organizational and social point of view, because people will get used to different things to meet their needs, and of this the market will have absolutely everything in mind. In the real estate market, therefore, the valuations will change, certainly also the strategies in the commercial field, which will determine new rules: now more than ever it will be necessary to look to the future, because another type of game is played >>.

- **RESIDENTIAL MARKET: WHAT CHANGES<<** The property has always had a fairly important and clear intrinsic value since the earliest times. Remember in the *old West*, when colonies and colonies of people went in search of luck. I am not talking about speculative and random search for gold, but about a more solid and secure form of investment or "land". This example means how ephemeral certain and even risky investments are, in spite of others who are absolutely always functional and with low probability of risk: << **a house is always a house**, it is worth a lot or it loses value, it will always be worth something> >, and by holding the property it can be used for different uses:
  - PERSONAL USE: we take into account that everyone needs a home, **used to reside and live**. The house can be "owned" or "long term rent". An interesting assessment to make is that paradoxically we could say that in Europe, or in the United States, << there are more houses than families >>.

In this case, the scenario will remain almost constant even today, because everyone will continue to need "a roof"; however, there may be a redistribution following covid-19.

- PROFITABLE USE: following the reasoning above, the owners, who can instead afford to count with significant savings and liquidity, taking advantage of the opportunities of the moment, have acquired and are acquiring more than one property and if sometimes this is used as second residence (for pleasure) or to carry out its commercial or industrial activity, in other cases the purpose is to invest to rent to a third party. In the case of the lease, therefore, we can say that the property was purchased in order to produce capital. These capitals would be "proceeds from *long, medium or short term* leases depending on the policies adopted by the owner. By defining **the long term as "stable typology",** the medium term as an "innovation", interesting to monitor, and the short term as "speculative" and following trends, we can assume that in the post Corona-virus it will continue and will be recommended "l 'long term rent".

- NO USE: I will surprise you by talking about this category because it is very interesting. << Who tells you that all properties serve some function? >>. They could only exist as a result of unplanned circumstances and be completely superfluous or even annoying (if we think that they must be maintained by paying taxes and maintenance to own them, without perhaps making use of them). We talk about wrong investments for example, never completed or unfinished, which therefore are not even in a condition to be rented, or we think about the inherited properties: the covid-19 or life in general, leave traces in 2020 of many deaths; many of these people were owners and therefore their heirs could either be new owners (and move from the condition of rent to that of having a first home) or they could simply inherit properties in unexpected form of which they do not know objectively what to do with them. These properties will be real **market opportunities**, in many cases because, once the emotional barrier is overcome, if careful commercial evaluations are made, there will be *a good sales motivation* and therefore market-compliant prices: in these conditions, many potential investors will want to win them for personal or investment purposes. It is difficult, although unfortunately sometimes it happens, to think that good properties remain unused to ruin inexorably over time: a wise owner will have to think how to use that capital before it devalues, because time deteriorates without remedy >>.

- **COMMERCIAL MARKET: WHAT CHANGES** << In this field, total uncertainty reigns, because the scale of what has happened is still to be measured. We previously mentioned a sort of natural selection, **where the best or those with the most financial resources will survive**, and also a sort of change in the structuring of certain points of sale and consequently of the type of property: if, for example, it took hold scale the automated selection and delivery of *supermarket shopping*, it is reasonable to think that small shops would suffer the latest lethal blow, and that food companies would dive into huge warehouses and warehouses organizing *Amazon*-style deliveries, instead of aiming for management of expensive stores located in strategic places. Natural selection and change of concept are in progress, therefore the effects of these changes cannot yet be predicted. However, we have also mentioned an old and expensive sector, which however cannot be expressed with today's technologies and cannot be performed in virtual form, because it has to do with the aggregation and production of "something done at the moment"; if you think about it, it is really the only thing that cannot have a corresponding virtual version. In fact, even if it is not the same, in extreme conditions you can see a football game virtually, or order any product and service, or make meetings and have friends and even a virtual girlfriend: but you will never "go to the bar virtually ". The *food & beverage* sector is not a type of trade that can be replicated in virtual form. Surely therefore, if on the one hand the classic shop risks disappearing due to the social changes or habits that people, restaurants, bars and hotels would assume, as "aggregation sellers and emotions" and a product that can only be used in a three-dimensional way "Live", they will continue their existence, albeit undergoing an important inflection of the numbers for the reasons already explained. However, there will also be an important exchange of sellers here who, due to the change in customer habits or to the accounts which are no longer favorable, will decide to sell, creating important market opportunities, in positions or situations that until some time before were unthinkable. The real "sharks" (expert investors), should be ready now with their capital to position themselves and take advantage of these market opportunities.

But what is the identikit of this type of investor?

It is absolutely a very expert and abundant profile, because the first thing that he will have very clear is that he will not start earning in the short term, but his is an investment over time: **he is only buying a good position at an advantageous price**, but it is very likely that, if he wants to assemble an activity today, he will have difficulties like everyone else, unless he again resorts to economic resources to build and position an activity as *market leader*. The beginner investor then? Someone from this other group will certainly move equally, even in unfavorable conditions, and will probably burn especially if they do not have specific skills in the business and economic reserves to deal with times of depression. All economic cycles offer market opportunities: the theme is "knowing how to read the score in advance" and moving accordingly >>.

CORONA VIRUS SEEN AS "GREAT MARKETING GENIUS"

Let's pretend for a moment that this strange enemy isn't completely against us, and let's study it as an economic example to steal its secrets in a totally neutral and selfless way.

Seen in this light, unconsciously covid-19, if we compared it to a company that wants to enter the market, it has moved with an absolutely unique and unrepeatable intelligence and strategy. Let's think about how silent he remained until the first days of 2020. He had organized himself and had been gathering all his forces probably for at least six previous months, without making any noise, << hiding and dressing himself with other names >> (when we thought it was a flu or in the worst case pneumonia). It was probably already present all over the world then, with the unconscious and often asymptomatic people, and it was multiplying, expanding and above all **positioning itself:** positioning is very important in an economic model, because it can discriminate the size, the times and the possibility to be successful. In the case of the virus, the positioning was intelligent and silent, and when he was now ready to launch his attack, he did it << from the best location, with the greatest possible strength, with speed, with the surprise effect, breaking the competition (ie leaving the various health services helpless) >> and rapidly consolidating itself as a reality that has dominated the market, that is our lives. In fact, when the right moment arrived, not only did he make himself known, but he also went to a more aggressive phase: he came to the "*boom*", where he routed everyone and fulfilled his purposes.

This, for example, is also a case of so-called << occult marketing >>, that is, without advertising. Advertising had to be done by the man later to understand what was happening: but the virus itself embarked on a perfect marketing strategy that quickly made it reach its goal.

I imagine that it is not exactly the most pleasant example I could use, but it certainly has an impact and can clearly explain how we should move in the market. Different strategies can be implemented (aimed at attracting attention such as advertising or occult as in the case explained), but the aim is always the same: the company must grow and expand according to a project and strategies well outlined and arrived at a certain point it has to "explode" to compete at full speed in the market. On the contrary, if you cannot reproduce this growth model, it is inexorably destined to decline because you are probably moving with inadequate marketing logic.

MARKETING ACTIONS IN COMMERCIAL ACTIVITIES

Different strategies can be implemented, but the winning point from which world and world is to vary the way or ways of proposing oneself, therefore to advertise and promote, while maintaining coherence in the strategy and direction, in the intrinsic characteristics of a given company, , with the aim of being able to correctly represent the main characteristics of the same and its proposal. So, meaning marketing as << **a set of strategies applied to achieve a predetermined purpose** >>, we will now analyze in general the fundamental characteristics of this type of planning, and then we will go on to list and explain the most suitable techniques for promoting in the 21st century, updated for technology and incisiveness.

It should be noted that it is not said that identical marketing actions produce the same results, discriminating over time, in the product and by the different companies. Often the non-expert eye does not understand why a strategy works for certain categories and for others not, and above all many times emulation is used as a "way out" to solve problems: it is in fact common sense that << a something that works very well for someone it could also work for others >>, but the opposite is also true, because it depends on the difference from the activities, each action has a different incisiveness according to certain *ad hoc* criteria.

Taking a concrete example in the *food and beverage* sector, it is not the same thing to promote a disco rather than a restaurant for business lunches: in the first case the goal is to sell "fun", therefore you have to create campaigns where the taste is enhanced to be together celebrating, transgression, movement, events; in the second case we need to be more concrete, quick and comfortable, because the goal is << to make it clear that good quality production is made at a fair price >>, which is the only thing that the recipients of that message are looking for : all the other factors that are secondary and typical of other types of restaurants, where people meet for pleasure and for the taste of eating and not purely for a need.

So setting up a wrong and not targeted marketing campaign on the objectives that are appropriate for your business is a waste of time and resources, therefore a cost. Also in this case there is a widespread "do it yourself" where many owners (apart from feeling decorators, entrepreneurs, cooks etc ... and excel in all these disciplines) even feel marketing experts: almost always these subjects simply end up by buying some random advertisements, certainly not implementing marketing policies! Remember that those who have been practicing in a certain business sector for many years probably know how to do all these things fairly well and have the experience to be able to at least distinguish the incisive actions from the lesser ones; but certainly those who do not have at least 15-20 years of experience, how can they think that it is so easy to replace a professional, from any of these fields, who always and only exercises his own subject and has repeated it in an innumerable number of occasions and in different contexts? Let's think about how vain, in the example taken to the extreme, could be to advertise "the convenience or speed of execution of cocktails" in a disco; with inverted parts, it is equally harmful to advertise the "great agglomeration of people and fun" in a business restaurant: even counterproductive therefore, in the second case where people are looking for something simple and disconnect a few minutes from work. Consistency, balance and clarity are essential in marketing, exactly as they were when we defined *Bar- staging* (harmony of message and elements): in fact, I consider *the point of sale* in marketing as an integral or fundamental part. But when you make the wrong advertisement at a store, it can lead to nothing or even a negative result. Think of a luxury restaurant for example, which has a certain level of customers, and has a high pro-medium price: why should it announce its activity in the "most popular newspaper in the city", if it does not work with large numbers, but with a niche of a certain social level? On the contrary, that niche of people, who would normally also pay a surcharge such as << taste of having something exclusive >>, could see this type of action as a decline or a downward path: it is the typical case in which even get to lose customers. It can be seen in this example, how a certain wrong line, too generalist, results in "mixing customers too much", that is, ruining their selection and uniqueness; in other cases there may be real changes in the type of user, and this of course can be conscious or unconscious, winning or absolutely losing, because at the mercy of events, and not instead the result of a strategy.

There is an old motto that says << in trade it is better that they speak badly rather than not speak >>. In a sense this was absolutely true in the 80s and 90s, but already with the new millennium and the internet (and subsequently with *social networks*), this concept has changed: before the comment, although negative it was dispersed and was considered totally random: rather than going as "anonymous", it was preferred to "be unpleasant", provided that people talked about a brand. This type of marketing action continues to be valid and very incisive for example in *gossip* or in the *reality TV* industry: it is the creation and projection of characters and situations, for which interest is created regardless of liking, because in any case it is created curiosity. However, already in the field of work and professionalism one must be very careful: with new technologies word of mouth is created artificially and can be a weapon in one's favor, but also give the coup de grace to any company, when negative . In fact today, almost all the large platforms dedicated to commerce, rather than to leisure in general, give anyone the opportunity to express themselves and therefore can tell the good and the bad of things, adding photos, comments and details, and thus creating media phenomena whereby << a place that is generally appreciated can become the best, while those who are not popular, can be completely sunk >>. In this case, if excellence cannot be achieved, it is better to go anonymously rather than poorly: from anonymity one could reprogram and start again; from widespread denigration, it is then necessary to reset everything, with an increase in costs and problems that cannot always be overcome.

In a world of *"like"* you therefore have the option << or not to get involved >> and to use the old commercial system (surely always a solid base, but not too competitive in certain fields nowadays), or get involved, but at that point you have to do it with the necessary investments and skills, in order not to have important negative repercussions. Once again, therefore, the "overturned concept" in business, so << it is not always true that those who spend less, really spend less >>.

Let's take a paradoxical example: today, we have all taken a plane in life. Why do you think they put two pilots for each plane plus the automatic pilot? The fairly simple answer is that << in an emergency, a beginner could hardly replace a pilot in something so delicate and technical >>. Professionalism is based on the fact that you pay a fee to someone to perform an action, which a layman would do with less quality, with more experience and a different management of unexpected events. So let's put ourselves in the perspective of being more critical with ourselves when we have a business and think sincerely << if we are spending a lot of money on simple advertising >> or if we are doing marketing research, because the costs can sometimes be similar, but the results certainly differ.

Clearly, even in marketing, it is necessary to distinguish who can help us express impact actions, in accordance with the type of company or goal we set ourselves: among the various professionals there are those who know how to deal with marketing in general, rather than others who know make certain specific and targeted actions on specific sectors. For example, in my personal experience, I as a real estate, I deal with marketing and marketing projects intended for the public "houses"; also expert in food and beverage and entertainment, I dedicate myself to the commercial activities of this sector; I would never dream of promoting marketing campaigns for a cosmetic industry, for example! The principles are obviously the same, but I would not have the knowledge of "how that type of work develops", nor of the strong points, nor of what exactly those specific customers want: *let's say that I could do it well to half*. Just like those who do not really and deeply know the "bar" sector and use the *"do it yourself"*, they can rarely or partially do well in promoting it. Using only 50% means "not optimizing a lot of potential" available. Think of a team game, if you were to pull from a rope: one team uses two arms, but the other uses only one; it seems quite obvious to me who will end up winning the game (regardless of who is the strongest or least), because there is one of the two *teams* that is not using its full potential.

In Spain, present throughout the online territory for consultancy (and available for live services only in certain territories, there is for example www.bares360.es with which I collaborate: this web page is the example of an agency strategic marketing for *food and beverage and intrateinment* companies, in the round: it offers all the most exclusive services for this type of sector, given the experience of its collaborators in this area. Newborn on the web, but made by people for years in this type business, ranging from the studied design of the venue, not only from an aesthetic point of view, but from the aforementioned functionality and optimization of spaces aimed at increasing revenues. We then move on to purely marketing services such as the creation of logos, advice on how to carry on web pages and social media, consultancy on company and personnel organization, event organization and much more. One of the most important branches, however, remains the sector of assistance for the sale of commercial activities or creation of companies to manage them: it is a very technical real estate niche but absolutely important for optimizing your investments; even in this section there is a course on << divestments of activities >> dedicated to real estate agents, which testifies to the need to provide "professional training" on these topics, with the aim of optimizing the work and entering all of them: these products (also the setting up of the store and the sale of the company) are important marketing actions and must be treated as such.

THOSE WHO DO NOT NEED MARKETING

This is a very hard and clear paragraph, where I would like to express my personal disappointment towards those who adhere to this "non-strategy", which is even worse in my personal ranking than those who "hurt marketing", but at least try.

Do not do marketing, it means not having a defined project aimed at achieving a result: that is, it means doing casual entrepreneurial activity, according to how it comes. It is quite evident that this does not agree with me, because if things are left "to chance" or follow a logic of taste, but not commercial, this can only produce a mediocre result. In response, therefore, to the issue we are analyzing, the casual, the inexperienced, or who would be better to change jobs before losing everything, do not do marketing. Of course, in life (unfortunately or fortunately) there are always exceptions, so even the most inept can sometimes achieve results, because kissed by luck and chance, or because it has significant economic resources that make up for other shortcomings. But in most cases, "non-control" or failure to plan is an it is an absolute source and the first sign of failure. There are instead subjects who boast or boast of not having to do marketing, because they have such a strong brand or a positioning that makes them unique and detached from the need to push.

We think of renowned and historic activities, which now automatically have a widespread word of mouth and therefore are totally free of interest in promotions. These realities are probably the only ones that can afford non-programming, because they live off their history's income, and therefore consider it more important to focus more on maintaining certain standards, rather than investing in growth. Admirable and respectable as a concept and absolutely truthful, even if they do not take into account one essential thing: time and change. These companies won't do marketing, but in the past their founder probably did it, and how! Thus they reached certain levels of excellence. We know, however, that the passage of time determines economic changes that are reflected in the industrial and commercial sphere, so it is not said that << what is good today also works tomorrow >>. It is quite plausible that these types of businesses are not concerned, at the present time, with applying marketing policies, but this obviously at the expense of any growth: over the years they will have to be ready when they have to change situations, for renew itself and apply policies aimed at relaunching its business to keep it competitive, in step with the times.ute source and first sign of failure.

There are instead subjects who boast or boast of not having to do marketing, because they have such a strong brand or a positioning that makes them unique and detached from the need to push. We think of renowned and historic activities, which now automatically have a widespread word of mouth and therefore are totally free of interest in promotions. These realities are probably the only ones that can afford non-programming, because they live off their history's income, and therefore consider it more important to focus more on maintaining certain standards, rather than investing in growth. Admirable and respectable as a concept and absolutely truthful, even if they do not take into account one essential thing: time and change. These companies won't do marketing, but in the past their founder probably did it, and how! Thus they reached certain levels of excellence. We know, however, that the passage of time determines economic changes that are reflected in the industrial and commercial sphere, so it is not said that << what is good today also works tomorrow >>. It is quite plausible that these types of businesses are not concerned, at the present time, with applying marketing policies, but this obviously at the expense of any growth: over the years they will have to be ready when they have to change situations, for renew itself and apply policies aimed at relaunching its business to keep it competitive, in step with the times.

MARKETING ACTIONS TO OPTIMIZE THE FOOD AND BEVERAGE SECTOR

As we said, marketing has basic rules that apply to all types of businesses, so the vast majority of what we will deal with now is widely applicable to other sectors: however I wanted to focus on my specialty and use my experience to talk about all the new technologies (and the classic system) available to companies, in this case of entertainment and catering: the new technologies are all those that apply since the advent of the internet, and therefore a lot has to do with the computer and a channeling of virtual means, aimed at increasing the value of the brand. The classic system is instead << all that series of systems that have always been used and that are old workhorses >>: a real solid base, which never expires from being important, but which if applied "alone", nowadays it may be insufficient to compete in the global world. The measure of all this also lies in the size of the market to which we refer: the more we talk about large markets, spaces and great competition, the more the need to differentiate and stand out is evident. In the small realities, however, the value of this whole study loses slightly strength at the expense of quality and interpersonal characteristics and empathy (which in any case never hurts to possess in any type of situation).

- **DIFFERENCES BETWEEN OLD SCHOOL AND NEW TECHNIQUES:** some of the dogmas of the old way of thinking was << being always present anyway >> and << the important thing is to make people talk about themselves >>. Claims also true, previously, but insufficient in 2020 because neither of them talks about programming. Maybe they could have been two good considerations at the advertising level, but today in any case they would be outdated, or better to integrate. In fact, not only must we be present, but we must choose the channel and be very competitive: the goal is to please and therefore project a perception of our business that attracts positive comments. It is a technological version of old school word of mouth, but the big news is that "people's opinions are in writing", easily available and accessible to everyone: they are called reviews. By now the largest platforms also use this system to characterize the product a little: especially in online shopping, where a person cannot see or touch with his hand, he often guides himself with the description of the product, with photos and videos and with comments from other people who have already purchased it. I state that personally I do not go crazy to buy based on the random opinion of others, and that I find it quite unpleasant when some friends << choose where to go to eat pizza looking at who has more stars >>. I confess, however, that the system is absolutely valid, even if it has advantages and disadvantages:

- ADVANTAGES: Among the advantages, there is certainly transparency for the customer, so when a person sees all negative reviews he can reasonably think that he is looking at the announcement of something that has potential problems. Another advantage, always for the customer, is the peace of mind to buy when he sees evaluations of positive experiences, and which therefore gives him added security to do the same. Another advantage is that of in-depth description, where someone who has been able to have small problems (and then solved them) explains their path so that a third party can be conscious and decide what to do. The advantages are also for the seller: positive reviews almost always coincide with the increase in sales, and positive opinions are a great marketing action, which, in a chain, develops a positive word of mouth and a positive impression that is reflected on the *brand*. Positive reviews also produce a replacement within the clientele of a company, and therefore a long-term growth, as well as the possibility of accessory sales (you were looking for an object, you mistakenly thought that that brand had it, but you discover others that interest you for other reasons, which you had not thought of): therefore the opportunity to diversify.

- DISADVANTAGES: when instead you do badly or have a bad marketing strategy, reviews can be a very unpleasant and annoying boomerang, which slows down growth, or even sinks the company in cases where this is not strong or to motivate them and to counter them or to be able to express such a high number of sales that they pass through without being perceived. In fact, in the case of many negative reviews, buyers will tend to curb their easy enthusiasm and deepen more. Sometimes they will give up. However, it is important to keep in mind that << all companies have negative reviews >>, even the most popular ones.

Let's take an example: could someone live now without "what's app"? It is the best mobile communication platform, the first in its history and the most widespread, capable of eliminating the use of ancient *text messages,* and has now become a *must* for almost everyone. Are there better applications? Maybe yes: they were born and there are several, but certainly less widespread and it will be very difficult for them to undermine this, as it continues to renew itself, strengthen its servers and grow. In fact one of the characteristics that belong to it are the absolute reliability of the program and the power of the servers. Other similar applications are perhaps more beautiful and nice, but not functional. Can you believe that "what's app", in reviews 1 to 5 of *online stores,* has a rating lower than 4? Incredible for something almost necessary first now, to communicate and work. Yet many negative reviews come, based on completely personal tastes and episodes. The disadvantage of a bad review is that of falling into the trap of the so-called *"haters",* that is, the discontents who sometimes exaggerate, leave their opinion in the comments. The comments, which can be both expressive and numerical to determine a *ranking,* will therefore depend on the fact that there are not too many negative reviews, which lower the average. This is why it is important nowadays to have a good marketing plan: there are few systems to counter negative reviews and depend on an accurate growth plan of your virtual image, which must have the possibility to counter them: technical arguments, in the case in which which are extended comments or the strength to disperse them having just as many positive ones, when there is a problem of evaluation. Think about the online market and how many times a seller prefers to refund their product, even when there are differences with the customer, when the opportunity to receive a negative review is feared: it could lose much more than the value it has sold us, if only they followed a couple of other negative reviews and lowered its reliability status. So you have to be very careful with marketing today, because unlike the old-fashioned word of mouth, it leaves a trace and directly and indirectly affects sales. In catering it is the same, raised to the nth degree! The old motto << people attracts people >> could be modernized with << positive reviews attract people >>, thinking of the various "tripadvisor", specific sites or even just the Google index, where everyone uses the same system. What not everyone knows that there is "the trick", so there are systems designed to be reviewed, and even real "review professionals" who do it just like a job and are dedicated to opening special accounts for do what is a real job, but which if done well can launch one product at the expense of another. The techniques vary unlike the various portals, but the principle is the same: << start being nice and others on the same wavelength queue >>. Many businesses do not even realize they are wrong or that they are going wrong, because by not taking care of their virtual image, they do not even notice they have many haters. Was it easier and more genuine before, with the old system of working? Maybe, or maybe not: we mentioned advantages and disadvantages;

what is certain is that the old systems, still very valid and milestones of commercial marketing, are not sufficient by themselves to compete at a high level.

- **MARKETING EVERGREENS** Still very present, especially in certain sectors, *flyers* **and signage** have always been two very powerful advertising vehicles. One arrives directly in people's mailboxes and can be differentiated in various formats such as flier (or booklet), business letter, private letter, etc ... It is undoubtedly always a powerful means, but has always had the obvious defect of high costs, due to of printing (even if digital printing has greatly reduced its prices today), but above all because of distribution, which is a job that can be done in a light and casual or professional way: the work done superficially is enough fast, and produces poor results for dispersion. In the case of a more expensive service with more guarantees, it is clear how much the costs may worsen; then we add the possibility that after such an important effort, the flyer may never reach the recipient's hands, as many buildings have a common "trash" for advertising (and I did not use the word trash at random!). The habit then of certain owners, even when leaflets were found in the mailbox, is to throw them in most cases without even reading them. So let's talk about an even worse case of not doing marketing: **<< think you have done it >>**, that is to say you have invested money and resources and seriously think you are doing something well, which instead is not so incisive. In large cities where the use of this technique in fact in past years was disproportionate, the incidence has dropped dramatically., Even if we record that it is always an old workhorse and if well implemented, with the right distribution, it is a evergreen.

The same goes for road signs for example. You have to differentiate yourself and certainly the road has always been one of the plausible places of visibility. This is also a workhorse, but certainly less incisive, in the presence of many other signs, because it is lost to the eye and sight. So it is important to do a study of << where it is profitable to place the signs >> in a strategic way according to the visibility and also according to the user you want to recall: << it seems a waste of resources to advertise women's beauty products in an industrial area, with mainly male density: net of the exceptions, there will never be numbers to pay back the investment, because the desired public is in other areas of the city >>. A very important example of signage is instead that of "repair or support" under the distinctive sign of a store. In cases where you approach the desired location, it is interesting to have indicators that warn you in advance and especially when you have a sign for location or technical limits, << hardly visible >>: it is absolutely necessary to consider investing in billboards in strategic positions and immediacy, which make up for this lack and enhance the store.

In the old school, we mention techniques relating to **newspapers, television and radio.** With the various differences in cost and type, they are always respectable evergreens, because many users access them daily. Unlike the first two vehicles, these are "placeable" and can be modulated on the type of customer (there are newspapers or radio for all age and social target groups). Or for example we think of TV with thematic channels, rather than with time slots: determining "when and how" therefore allows you to be more incisive and start skimming the majority of the desired audience. What I would like to highlight most is the incidence of local radio and television, which is absolutely important for a company. Think of the best restaurant in our city: what interest would it have to go on national television to advertise itself, and pay very high commissions? It could have only one narcissistic purpose, but from an economic point of view it would be totally too onerous and little incident. On the other hand, in local television, it would access practically all the desired users, i.e. that of its own city, and could discriminate the interest groups according to schedules and programming, because using sports, costumes and news services, this type of means of communication, with the its schedule, is very attractive for those who want to keep up to date on news related to their territory: this will also be the preferred audience to attract with our corporate marketing.

Another great classic is the posting on **buses and taxies** in large cities: it is a widespread and always current system, but which, depending on the number of reproductions or sizes, can be very expensive in terms of costs. and therefore the opportunity must be carefully considered before deciding to apply this type of policy, which I consider very aggressive and important.

We could go on for hours making other examples, but the concept is that the old school represents everything that has always been done in terms of visibility more than anything else physics, that is something that you can touch or move but that has always found in the big limit of the costs of production or service its great brake, in the past often generating exorbitant accounts under the budget item "advertising": for this reason, there was in the past among the entrepreneurs the widespread and perhaps then truthful opinion, that << advertising is not measurable >>, that is, it has to be done, but you never know what it really brings you! Modern marketing concepts, especially with the spread of advertising on the web, have radically changed this concept.

- **MARKETING 2020** The advent of the internet shocks the world since the beginning of the new millennium, but nobody at the beginning would have thought that we would have come so far when we installed the first modem years ago << which made whistles and gargles >> and was very slow at point to leave us desperate for minutes... waiting to see a normal website. Today with modern technologies, and super browsing speed, we watch films and programs live or recorded, we make video conferences and (consciously or unconsciously) we receive continuous marketing messages all day long by everyone: therefore the potential visibility of this action is absolutely constant and extremely powerful, considering that by now we have it on the computer at work all day and on the cell phone in the private sector, even at night. So the spreading and breaking down of borders is one of the great achievements of virtual marketing, capable of reaching indiscriminately everywhere and reaching anyone with well-applied strategies. Another of the important achievements concerns the reduction of costs: the internet is virtual, and therefore it does not require production and limits the service to a minimum. Even modern techniques allow the user himself to "self-manufacture" an ad and launch it, paying practically only a commission. Lately producing advertising has become so easy and cheap that it is within everyone's reach, so much so that one of the first disadvantages of this has been the loss of the desire to invest capital in advertising. We have therefore gone from the realization of expensive campaigns with billboards and magnificent initiatives, to admitting only free advertising for our company, trusting in the various facebook and similar applications (often totally free), with the conviction and the purpose that these actions are sufficient to promoting the business': in reality they don't even know each other very well (remember that commercial use is much more complex than private use) and it is often another example in which we think of advertising incisively, but we are just getting there to a small part of the market share, or to a few acquaintances and friends.

Indeed, one of the consequences of the popularity of the network is that anyone is online, privately or commercially, and therefore a series of related problems arise that are not always known. The first is technical, that is, the various social media applications allow the display of a free advertisement only to a certain number of users according to an algorithm: that is, they are excellent for organizing a private party for a few dozen people (use for to which they were expressly conceived), but to fill a stage they are insufficient if used in standard form. It is therefore necessary to apply certain techniques to make them more preforming and enter into the perspective of understanding that << the jump from super expensive advertising in the 90s to zero-cost advertising in 2015 is too large for a commercial activity >>.

We must continue to invest and have results and apply the correct actions of a targeted marketing aimed at optimizing revenues. In fact, only through investments and certain actions of an important quality, it is possible to stand out from the crowd. If everyone is on the internet, this means that you have to emerge and differentiate yourself from others, because obviously the daily attention has limits and the mind of the average user is constantly bombarded with messages all day and every day. We will now go into detail to see all the most important techniques, to highlight a company by using the new generation of virtual commercial marketing and proposing the updating of certain classic concepts readapted to 2020 with the updated version and the application of new technologies.

- **COMPANY LOGO:** everything must start with the logo. The logo is the expression of a brand, summarized in a drawing or an inscription. It must identify who we are and what we do, be attractive and captivating and must give a sense of continuity because it will appear in all the marketing actions we will do. It is a bit like the business card of the business, but in a virtual version applicable to everything: newspapers, television, internet stocks, signs, price list, even uniforms and corporate work tools. To the customer's eye, he will always identify the company, first reminding him that it exists and then why he should use it. The best logos are simple. They can be colored and absolutely must be original; sometimes there is the creation of surreal logos by companies of the highest order and level: in these cases, the virtual image that they will project is compromised.
- **SIGN OF THE POINT OF SALE** The sign characterizes the store and the message we address to the public about our product. The visibility is very important which not only depends on the size, but also and above all on the "visual field" of a customer with

respect to the situation (in a pedestrian street where people move slowly, different techniques are applied, rather than on a sliding highway); to take into account also the night and day factor where new technologies absolutely help us both for a typical aesthetic taste, but also for the flexibility and increased visibility that they allow. It is always advisable to include the logo and a simple but impactful message and to use very simple characters that are not crowded together, because as we said earlier, the world now moves at such a speed that complex things often get lost in sight.

- **WEB PAGE:** Years ago, as soon as this novelty was introduced and cleared through customs, it was easy enough to make companies understand that they had to have a page that talked about them in a widespread way, that explained their products and put them in contact with their users. There are different types of web pages, and I'm not talking about colors or graphics, where there is a whole art and special professionals, but I'm talking about types of use:

- ADVERTISING WEB PAGE: the classic example is that of the restaurant that publishes its *menus*, location, a few photos and therefore wants a customer to find his page so that he can get information and be curious to visit the store.
- SUBSTITUTE WEB SITE OF THE POINT OF SALE: the most typical example is *Amazon*, a giant of online commerce, where you can buy anything you would buy in a hypermarket, and in fact replaces it completely, except for the food sector (but they have the structure and the network to do it in the future: do you think that if there were new covid-19-style diseases, with all that it represented, they wouldn't think about managing a food sale? In any case, if not them, there are others of smaller size that they do and are empowering it).
- WEB CURRICULUM PAGE: practically it is a professional page where a professional or worker offers his own person and makes himself available for services. - PURE WEB PAGE: online activity page or online service. The most typical example are thematic pages dedicated to videos, for example: free of charge

by advertising *banners* or paid by subscription, they perform their function directly from their virtual platform. All these models and others are absolutely essential to carry out your business, but they all lack marketing: it is not enough to have a web page. Let's go back to the example of << believing you are doing an action >> which, however, is actually not incisive. A web page is of very little use if it is not easily encountered and nowadays finding things in the chaos of internet information is really complicated. Having a web page and then not applying certain actions to enhance it, is like having a restaurant located in a super secondary street that is very difficult to find. Clearly the potential audience changes. The first thing to explain is that therefore the web page must be indexed on search engines, through keywords and other marketing techniques that will increase its visibility. If people start to find it, and secondly to find it attractive, the visibility numbers will increase in algorithmic form because the various search engines always favor the best web pages, at the expense of the less searched ones. This is fundamental, because many times it is the fine line between success or failure. With different logics and algorithms, it is a bit like what happens with real estate portals when you put your house on sale: do you think it is important to remain visible at the top of the list of ads or is it the same to have a poorly indexed ad? The answer is that sometimes when it is very specific or very niche they find it anyway, perhaps with more effort, but it doesn't change much. But in matters of large numbers, a lot changes! In the same way, index your website and have it present in the first pages of the search engines enhances both the site itself and your company and therefore makes the marketing action undertaken effective.

Another discriminant is the content of the site. Again, I'm not just referring to aesthetic issues. I was the first to make the mistake of << wanting to put everything >> in the past many times. It is obvious that the online site of a *technological e-commerce* must put all its televisions, all its computers, all the household products that it holds, and the more things it does, the better it is: this is because it is selling a "product list". But in most cases the product is only one or they are few and when creating the site there is a tendency to write a lot, and therefore useful information is often lost. The web page must be easy and intuitive and present essential products and services. It must have simple but attractive graphics and must have cohesion with the physical store if there is one.

To make up for these shortcomings and also for the purpose of selling, the concept of **landing pages** has recently been introduced which are nothing more than other related web pages, which often refer to the main web page, but created specifically for the purpose of selling. In other words, since the website is very dispersed and must contain a lot of information, pages that are easier to index are launched which recall the main details, but which are graphically even more intuitive and minimalist, which have a clear message and which attract the customer. Maybe promoting a gift or with some absolutely commercial artifice. These obviously are indexed in turn in search engines through marketing techniques, but above all their use is becoming particularly interesting in the commercial application of social media, where attention is always undermined by too much information and there is a need for very simple impact.

- **SOCIAL MEDIA:** Similarly to the fact that everyone uses "what's app", everyone knows today what facebook, twitter, instagram and all the various *social media* variants on the market are, which differ in technology and potential audience. Social media are collectors of people who allow them to stay in touch with each other and interact virtually by writing texts, publishing photos and videos and with dozens of other more complex and varied functions depending on the genre. The first, most famous and known is *Facebook*, which is now present in practically all our homes. It was undoubtedly one of the greatest innovations of the past twenty years because it improved communication and allowed us to break down social barriers, which until a few years ago seemed insurmountable. It is evident that, as in everything, on the other hand, it has also brought many problems, such as the birth of the famous *"fake news"*, that is, the fake, fictional, distorted news, or real interpersonal conflicts, for the most varied reasons. On the other hand, however, it was also a very powerful commercial vehicle because those who understood in time the application and importance of these advertising media, studied the algorithm and understood how to optimize marketing campaigns in order to reach more people: the same announcement can reach only 1000 people instead of one hundred thousand depending on the policies adopted. Unfortunately, in this case the *do it yourself* has always had the perception of reaching everywhere in the world (and potentially it is because there really are no barriers), but the creators of the algorithm, once seen the widespread expansion of the platform, they had to put some restrictions, understanding first that for example << who organized a popular concert in the center of Madrid, it was useless that it was visible in New York >> and in a more restrictive form, that it was visible even in the south of Spain it is wasted.

Potentially a New Yorker, for his part, can always search and find this event, exactly like all the events published in the world, in any location they are, however, unless he has a direct relationship with the organizer or an acquaintance , or is not interested in that niche, in theory "does not interest him" and therefore it is right that he does not see it. (this is the sense of the facebook algorithm). So the free and standard use of Facebook, even if it can give us the feeling of being able to get everywhere, is actually limited: we are "targeting" only our own circle of friends, while the other potentially interested users get lost in the sea of information of the thousands of proposals present.

To remedy this type of operation, commercial pages have been introduced in Facebook, with the aim of allowing the registration of people interested in a certain type of activity and therefore of getting in touch with them directly. Probably other platforms have other artifices or other logics, but the common sense is the same: as for the web page, the problem of appearing in a container where there are a lot of messages, is absolutely a priority to solve. It is not plausible to think that a potential customer sees every single publication or every single ad: here marketing techniques intervene to improve the charm of the ads rather than the effectiveness of the advertising campaigns. The first objective always remains that << the greatest number of people see the existence of their ad and secondly that they decide to read it >> because it has attracted his attention. Let's go back to talking about the *landing pages* that you can insert in a text ad with the aim of converting that attention received into a sale, or videos or very attractive images that must come to produce the attention of new customers. The big news is that so far we have talked about all this, but practically at no cost (free facebook service), that is in the standard mode: the problem with this type is that it is very limited, because the situation is not the manager has it, but it depends randomly on a customer who decides to subscribe to his page or to his personal circle of friends. Among other things, these potential users are not yet considered as "real customers" because they may simply be curious or not have a specific interest in "buying" (remember that the product, or objective, can be physical, but also simply advertise your company or professionalism). So the conversion rate (ie the ability to transform a contact into a sale) is very low, and we could therefore speak of << a lot of noise for nothing >>, with slight effects on the diffusion of certain messages or of a certain level of advertising ', but absolutely not relevant in positive to create revenues. On the contrary, it could instead attract haters, and then not have the numbers or the strength to be able to deny them and it can be very harmful for our company.

How can social media become a weapon of advantage for a company and produce revenues? The so-called *organic public* is a good starting point to measure yourself at the beginning and understand the market logic, but it is not at all sufficient and alone will never produce, as far as it may present high interest numbers, real revenues . To optimize the social tool on a professional level, the only answer is to invest and plan, then marketing.

<< When ever in the history of commerce something that is free produces revenues and earnings? >>. Answer << never! >>, word already included in the question.

If you do not pay you can survive, earn something, but in the vast majority of cases it is totally insufficient to handle the marketing of an entire company. Advertising must be paid for and therefore, remembering the old school models, you just have to be happy to pay so little, but you have to access the paid step, because otherwise you will not advance. Returning to the example of Facebook, there is a paid service which is precisely the Facebook ADS, which are nothing more than taking the same ad and proposing it in a completely different, selected market; depending on the parameters that we will decide, it allows us to get the message to only certain categories. Another great innovation, speaking of the price, is that everyone decides how much to invest for each ad. So big news ', because' now we are aware that by paying a little we can go to decide who gets our announcement and who doesn't: we can discriminate the age, gender, area of residence, the particular interests of this person and therefore direct us to an ideal model customer.

There will be statistical elements to check the progress and quality of your marketing actions and conversion rates, then measure the effectiveness of advertising, which with the old school methods was indecipherable. It is really well done and it is a powerful marketing tool. There is only one small and long-standing old problem << the letter arrives in the mailbox, but seeing that the customer is advertising it throws it away >>: we could therefore also reach the perfect customer, but if we get there with an incorrect message either trivial or not incisive, the effort will have been useless: therefore again to underline the importance of the *landing pages* or anything we send to our end user: it must be simple but of quality, and differentiate and must convert the action for sale or in the goal that is proposed.

- **YOU TUBE**

    For You Tube, I sincerely feel like making a separate speech and not locking it up in the social category. In a certain sense it is, because people can interact through comments, but on the other hand it was born as a platform for music videos and becomes so popular that it is now converted into the most popular container of any video in the world. In fact, there are now videos of all kinds, from small film clippings to the entire film, from music videos to the complete discography of an author; but pay attention to the absolutely innovative advertising application: this was for example one of the most incisive vehicles of the disclosure of what is *ad hoc* advertising, that is, the one that comes out of the margin of a daily and normal action, like looking for a song on the internet, and almost unconsciously "pay" it by being subjected to an advertisement at the beginning of the service or appearing to the side during. There are many famous sites, with heavy visitor traffic, where *advertising banners* are published, which are the real sponsors of those services. To access it there are ADS payment policies that must necessarily be a marketing study: there are *"pay-per clicks"*, or other devices, for which to personalize a real campaign. And even more interesting is the << intuitive system of interest >>: to date, search engines and *cokiees* (automatic messages rich in information, which are sent to the search engines on the most visited sites) are now possible advertising campaigns that act << on the interests and memory >> of the virtual navigator. For example, if a person searches on the website of Ikea, the global furniture giant, a product of his online store, this will be classified in some way, and remains in memory, so it is possible that, the result of elaborate campaigns of marketing, we find ourselves the next day reproposed that same object or other similar in some banner, when we go to visit any other site of our interest (sometimes in the same category, but sometimes even in terms of fun or that have nothing to do with see with a purchase). Imagine which advertising channel is more impactful and user-friendly than a film, music and various interests platform like You Tube! So an entrepreneur could intervene at the marketing level by creating intelligent and ultra-modern campaigns with these systems and always discriminating the type of customer, and having control over the number of ads seen and the number of clicks.

In any case, one of the other most interesting uses from a commercial point of view is the so-called *Tutorial* or video guide, where sector experts publish videos that are often very useful on **"how to solve a problem":** there are simple cooking videos to the more complex, mechanical; from videos of professionals explaining certain situations to videos of companies explaining the stages of a production. It is therefore extremely important from a strategic point of view for two main reasons: the first is that a truly capable person can create a video that illustrates his professionalism, and through the tool of offering a free demonstration, accessible to all, attracting new customers. . The second thing is for advertising purposes only to make yourself known, attract a large number of audiences and even in some cases monetize directly from the web, thanks to the great visibility that is then remunerated. In fact, not everyone knows that You Tube is owned by Google (the most important search engine in the world) and therefore its videos are normally highly indexed and pushed if they receive visits, which for Google is synonymous with being interesting.

Google and Facebook, to date, are the two most powerful *search bars* in the world, because they count with the most detailed information of potential customers and have the best technology available on the market, as well as applications. The problem then, here as before, is to emerge from the chaos of messages and videos uploaded to the platform, and often we find ourselves finding that a beautiful and super interesting video has very few views, at the expense of one made much worse , which covers the same topic and has thousands and thousands of views. So how do you achieve certain results? You Tube, like all platforms, has an interest that its customers are constantly connected, therefore it rewards the amount of videos uploaded: the experts themselves confirm that hardly anyone who publishes a single video can make large numbers: they therefore promote the self-supply of the platform inviting to make videos. This thing, on the one hand attracts very competent people who offer interesting technical or curious videos, artistic expressions and very useful advice. On the other hand, it attracts instead the lust for protagonism of certain other characters, who with the objective of "notoriety" (or with the objective of << doing a job, which they often cannot do >>), produce videos that are totally questionable in terms of quality and content . These subjects obviously lower the average quality of video productions and disperse "the potential to be seen" by others: unfortunately there is no taste filter, so it is obvious that they are the rules of the game. As if this were not enough, the junk videos are very popular and very popular with the public and even almost for a sort of "reverse justice", they tend to get a lot of views, and therefore these characters continue very willingly in their production. Speaking of real estate, for example, this is what happens sometimes with videos of excellent professionals, who make absolutely truthful and useful market surveys, at the expense of someone who "claims to be real estate" and sometimes says quite the opposite, without meaning , and therefore confusing the correct work of the other, moreover. How to combat this phenomenon and make the public understand that it is "the good one"? First of all by investing, because exactly as it happens with Facebook, there is a paid plan to push your production, connected to the *Google ADS:* then with the strength of the numbers, exhibit a different credibility of your videos (I know it seems a trifle to have to pay to stand in front of someone perhaps inept, but unfortunately freedom and ease of publication has this price). Secondly, there is a keyword strategy that You Tube allows to implement and that reads according to its algorithm. Understanding the keywords to enter to position yourself, so that a possible customer finds us before others, is essential and makes the difference. Thirdly, there is the usual system of reviews and comments that could give indications on good and less good videos, but unfortunately, in this case they are currently filterable, so it is plausible that the subjects we were talking about hide them. Warning: I say that it is very sad, in terms of numbers, because with a sensationalist video, a subject could get to have many clicks, but obviously then a potential customer will watch the video and make an opinion: it is evident that at that point he will understand if the video or the character has no quality (but the click will already be counted), and at this point he will probably interrupt the vision, looking for another more professional one: clearly this strategy brings fame, but does not convert potential customers into real customers. As a professional, I prefer a few qualified and selected clients, who see a video of mine and maybe convert into a real client, rather than having thousands of registered fans, perhaps most disgruntled, who do not lead me to monetize anything even over time. Quality always pays, in the end, and therefore also "who publishes" must then decide what << job to do in life >>: whether the entertainer or the professional; in fact, in the long run, these phenomena tire and people lose interest, or they completely lose credibility when they demonstrate scarce content, or very rough knowledge of the topics covered, or bizarre theories. So personally to companies and investors I recommend quality videos, with marketing techniques applied, not focused on sensationalism, but absolutely professional, aimed at a business purpose, demonstrating the seriousness and goodness of the product. The **advantages** of investing in this type of platform are that, often, it is the user who enters here looking for a solution, and not the company to go looking for it; moreover, the videos are very strong in terms of communication: larger than a photo, but less dispersive than a brochure. In a modern system everything is very visual, and few people read, at least in this type of situation: a quick and impactful solution is sought. They are also modular, being able to vary aside from the topics, the more serious style, the use of audio or subtitles; Finally, let's not forget the advantage and convenience of "showing something" in real time, while the user emulates us on the other side of the screen. If we then learn to invest, use the correct *keywords* and invest in ADS, managing to have some fashion videos, our business could take advantage of a visibility that is completely exponential and therefore grow visibly.

- **SALES LIST or CARD:** leaving the internet, I would like to approach something that was part of the old school, but has undergone an absolutely current "re-adaptation" over the years and connects to the aforementioned *bar-staging*, and looking for consistency and homogeneity between the product-point of sale and communication.

From time immemorial a company in any sector has always had a list of its products, and for this reason the issue and the importance of having an order and an interesting variety of products to offer is well known. However, its application is even more interesting, for example in the restaurant sector, where I believe it should be contextualized in a modern concept. In fact, what once represented only << the list of dishes offered in a restaurant >>, today, unless we are talking about *elite* niches, or family management, must be studied in order to optimize costs - receive, through a study that certainly has in its foundations << the best quality 'at the most accessible price possible >>, to produce large numbers. It must also represent the spirit and character of the store. From this perspective, therefore, composing a good card or list becomes a marketing action, and not just an instrumental and practical use of a list. The greatest cheffs /television entrepreneurs, in their dedicated thematic programs, when they go to propose a "change of image of a local", also and above all work on the "paper", with attention to the demand / offer, to the capacity of the point sale of being able to express a certain production, with price logics, with novelty and contextualization logics on the site: if we think in England of Gordon Ramsey (from the "Cucine dell'Inferno" program) and in Spain of Alberto Chicote

("Pesadilla en la cocina"), are two connoisseurs, who with a very professional *team*, intervene on the premises from an aesthetic, marketing and therefore also and above all by changing the product offer, to give a new personality to the various catering sites. Among other things, we remember that "this is my personal specialization", and for this I collaborate with sites like www.bares360.es where precisely this type of marketing and services is promoted.

Anyone can study a "card"; but studying a card that can convert into sales, to optimize revenues is a much more elaborate and complex job, exactly like all the other techniques analyzed so far, which are available to everyone in a free or intuitive way, but certainly have a different "firepower" if a professional uses them.

- **ORGANIZATION OF EVENTS AS A MARKETING PLAN:** previously we had proposed the example of a room with an entertainment room, which organizes events, with a precise strategy of increasing the turnout and brand value. Most companies use events for the sole purpose of attracting people and making themselves known, or increasing revenue at certain punctual moments. But seen from a commercial perspective, it is necessary to think that every single fan of an artist or a show can convert into a potential real customer, and in turn generate new customer flows once loyal, because he will recommend us to others. Seen in this light therefore there are very interesting commercial choices to be made on the style of the shows, rather than on the names of the artists and obviously the cost: in fact, each typology could have a different audience for economic availability or age, and therefore it is interesting use the organization of events to plan a growth strategy over time aimed at training a certain type of customer, akin to our business, and not only use it as a mere *"one-night"*, in order to make an interesting collection. In these cases, there is also a need to reflect on ticket payment policies and services and accessory spaces to generate revenues: the location of the food area, the beverage area, for example. Sometimes I happened to see in my long experience of the premises, perfect concerts full of people, but that the organizer was unable to convert correctly into sales, due to lack of organization, because overwhelmed by the unexpected number of users, for the incorrect arrangement of the sensitive points to join the collection. It is therefore very important to plan something that attracts the public, to study what kind of audience then and how to be able to optimize revenues by giving them the main service and the accessory ones, and all this aimed at both making a great income, but also cultivating something important over time, which replicated, which increases the value of the company and the brand.

- **HUMAN RESOURCES AS A SOURCE OF MARKETING:** all of us have happened to walk through a commercial area and find young people who come close and offer us to visit a place to sell products: the classic *PR*, public relations, that promote the store in the street or in the more advanced form of the night that organize parties and events in discos, moving quantities of people and bringing them to the store. The lowest common denominator is "attracting attention" and is the best known and most widespread form of human resource marketing. Obviously, these supports have a cost and can be more or less valid, depending on the period, the capabilities and what you want to promote. However, there are other human resources suitable for promoting a shop that in a certain sense could do so without increasing costs: the employees. In fact, employees are one of the natural sources of corporate marketing, as they are often "the face that speaks to the public" and therefore they are in all respects the subjects who must send absolutely positive messages and aligned with the style of the company in which they work. Let's think for a moment about what a powerful marketing action is << wearing a uniform with the company logo >> for each employee. Creating uniforms of this kind, at the beginning, appears to be an avoidable cost, but in the end it is a very forward-looking marketing operation because customers constantly display the company logo and it remains etched in the mind, and people passing by (think of the example of a promenade) they see the logo, maybe the smile of those who represent the company and they remember and maybe they are attracted to try the experience. Then we think of "word of mouth" and the friendships of the employees themselves: these can, with their good work, ensure that a company has the constant sap of customers, who are loyal to the good work done by the person who exercises in the store. On the contrary, it is clear that this can negatively affect when you have unmotivated or even incapable employees. So also the selection of human resources, by gender, age, ability, attitude, can be an important marketing choice because it produces direct consequences at work and indirect from the point of view of communication that in the long run affect the store's revenue. There has always been the old balance of imbalance between employee and employee, and sometimes one or the other have complaints about the other party: finding the perfect balance is a difficult business programming action, which but it is necessary: therefore, flexibility is needed on both sides, for a single common purpose, which is that of the corporate good. In fact, both when things are going well have "to gain". If instead they go wrong, probably everyone has to lose. We never underestimate this type of marketing, because it is fundamental, and above all a good employee applies it in a natural way just by doing his job well, so it is absolutely not an additional cost. (A bad employee on the contrary generates losses and problems).

It doesn't matter if you take the best photos or videos if nobody sees them!

CHAPTER 4: CONCLUSIONS

During our analysis we dealt with all aspects concerning residential and commercial investments, with special attention in the latter case to commercial activities and the category that most represents them in terms of diffusion and popularity, namely the food and beverage and revenueinment sector.

So we talked about the investor and all he needs to know to buy well and build a business that is profitable and that can provide him with income over time, differentiating unstable investments from safer ones.

Throughout this process, we wanted to underline the importance of programming, of serious and devoted application to the business system, conducted in a non-casual form, but inspired by good ideas, supported by facts and professional actions, aimed at increasing a make it strong and useful. We then definitely defined the do-it-yourself, intended as improvisation, an attempt to save or disorder, as a very widespread, but very negative element since in the long run it does not allow to build the foundations for stable and profitable work, giving only a few benefits immediately, and on the contrary, often generating a series of problems and inconsistencies that lead the company to make less than hoped for.

On the contrary we have promoted the action of a few but good professionals of the various professions: it is not secondary to differentiate the really good ones from the mediocre ones, but once done, we have motivated what are the important values that these professional figures should have, and above all done a portrait of how an investor can recognize and evaluate them and the knowledge they should have.

Because... let's not forget that the common goal of all this path is that of the company asset and the optimization of the investment, so you must know how to recognize the right investment, be able to grab it, mount a system that is profitable and succeed to sell: a lot of specializations required, therefore, for a very long laborious and complex job, which if it runs smoothly in any of these phases, turns into less profitable than expected, even to the point of being negative. In this sense, we find at the end, the real difference between the *do it yourself* and a professional support system for an investor: provided that both situations can lead to success or failure, as the case may be, what is certain that a self-styled allologist who "arranges himself" can only go so far; but an entrepreneur with vision and organization, who knows how to make use of his knowledge, and where he wants to optimize his revenues, with the help of valid professional advice, always has an additional weapon, as well as a meter of comparison. Indeed, I would say that this is precisely the point: it will be able to express a clearly more targeted and broader firepower, and it will certainly achieve the objectives it had set itself and perhaps even go further.

www.ingramcontent.com/pod-product-compliance
Lightning Source LLC
Chambersburg PA
CBHW071352210526
45465CB00001B/65